starting out:
Sicilian
grand prix attack

GAWAIN JONES

EVERYMAN CHESS

Gloucester Publishers plc   www.everymanchess.com

First published in 2008 by Gloucester Publishers plc (formerly Everyman Publishers plc), Northburgh House, 10 Northburgh Street, London EC1V 0AT

Copyright © 2008 Gawain Jones

British Library Cataloguing-in-Publication Data
A catalogue record for this book is available from the British Library.

ISBN: 9781 85744 5473

Distributed in North America by The Globe Pequot Press, P.O Box 480, 246 Goose Lane, Guilford, CT 06437-0480.

All other sales enquiries should be directed to Everyman Chess, Northburgh House, 10 Northburgh Street, London EC1V 0AT
tel: 020 7253 7887; fax: 020 7490 3708
email: info@everymanchess.com: website: www.everymanchess.com

EVERYMAN CHESS SERIES (formerly Cadogan Chess)
Chief Advisor: Byron Jacobs
Commissioning editor: John Emms
Assistant editor: Richard Palliser

Typeset and edited by First Rank Publishing, Brighton.
Cover design by Horatio Monteverde.
Printed and bound in Great Britain by Clays, Bungay, Suffolk.

Contents

Bibliography   4

Introduction   7

1   2...Nc6 3 f4 g6 4 Nf3 Bg7 5 Bc4   13

2   2...Nc6 3 f4 g6 4 Nf3 Bg7 5 Bb5   29

3   2...d6 3 f4   68

4   2...e6 3 f4   87

5   Other Second Moves for Black   114

6   2...Nc6 3 Bb5: Introduction   128

7   2...Nc6 3 Bb5 Nd4   146

Index of Variations   167

Index of Complete Games   173

Bibliography

Books

Anti-Sicilians: A Guide for Black, Dorian Rogozenko (Gambit 2003)
Chess Openings for White, Explained, Lev Alburt, Roman Dzindzichashvili and Eugene Perelshteyn (CIRC 2006)
Fighting the Anti-Sicilians, Richard Palliser (Everyman 2007)
Sicilian Grand Prix Attack, James Plaskett (Everyman 2000)
The Road to Chess Improvement, Alex Yermolinsky (Gambit 1999)

Periodicals and Software

British Chess Magazine
ChessBase Magazine
Chess Informant
ChessPublishing.com
Mega Database 2007
The Week in Chess
UltraCorr database

Acknowledgments

I would like to thank the many people who have helped me in the writing of this book. I'd like to thank my mother, Tanya Jones, for proofreading and my father, Martin Jones, for helping me with the computer side, in particular helping out when my computer's hard disk failed just before the book's completion! My thanks go to Thomas Rendle for double checking my variations and giving me useful advice; Richard Palliser and John Emms for sending me useful sources and helping out with the technical side of the book and a special thanks to John for being lenient about the deadline! A final thanks goes to Angus Dunnington, my former coach, who first taught me the Grand Prix Attack.

Introduction

The Grand Prix Attack is a complete repertoire against the Sicilian, Black's most popular reply to 1 e4. It provides an aggressive system: White's aim is simply to direct his pieces towards Black's kingside and open up Black's king, often with a well timed f4-f5 break. If Black prevents this plan, then White can often switch to a more positional theme, attacking Black's queenside pawns or exploiting weak central squares.

The Grand Prix Attack is named after the many English players, such as Mark Hebden and Dave Rumens, who used it successfully in weekend tournaments in the 1970s and '80s throughout the United Kingdom. White avoids the mountains of theory on the main lines and forces Black to play in his type of position. The opening was extremely successful and was then taken up by the world's top players, such as current World Champion and number one, Vishy Anand. There are only a few lines that White needs to learn; the rest of the positions can be played using general principles.

History of the move order

White used to play f2-f4 on move two, i.e. **1 e4 c5 2 f4**. However, the reply **2...d5!** **(Diagram 1)** is good for Black as the following game samples show:

3 exd5

3 e5?! cannot be advised: White gives away important squares and allows Black's pieces to develop easily. 3 Nc3 and 3 d3 are playable but seem to give inferior versions of positions we can get from 2 Nc3. Therefore, nowadays, the games normally begin 1 e4 c5 2 Nc3, to stop Black's ...d7-d5, and this book will only concentrate on this move order.

3...Nf6

Black can also recapture straight away with 3...Qxd5. After the text White can retain his extra pawn, but it allows Black a great deal of compensation; for example:

a) 4 Nc3 Nxd5 5 Nf3 Nc6 doesn't promise White any advantage.

b) 4 c4 e6! 5 dxe6 Bxe6 6 Nf3 Nc6 7 Nc3 Bd6 (7...Be7!? is also interesting, planning ...Qc7 and ...Rd8 to cover d4) 8 d4 cxd4 9 Nxd4 0-0 10 Nxe6 fxe6 11 Be3 Qe7 12 Qf3

Bb4 13 Be2 e5 leaves Black having all the fun, A.Rosich Valles-G.Kasparov, Barcelona (simul) 1988.

c) 4 Bb5+ Bd7 (4...Nbd7 is also possible) 5 Bxd7+ Qxd7 6 c4 e6 7 Qe2 Bd6 8 d3 (or 8 dxe6 fxe6 9 d3 0-0) 8...0-0 9 dxe6 fxe6 10 Nf3 Nc6 11 0-0 **(Diagram 2)** and now 11...Rae8, as in N.Short-G.Kasparov, Paris (rapid) 1990, or 11...e5!? gives Black good counterplay.

Diagram 1 (W)	**Diagram 2 (B)**
Disrupting White's set-up	Black has good counterplay

These lines may be playable for White, but Black's position is more enjoyable. Generally, when playing the Grand Prix Attack, we want to be attacking. With 2...d5 Black counterattacks and this is not really in the spirit of our opening, and may not even promise White any advantage.

Plans in the Grand Prix

The ultra-aggressive kingside attack

White plays Qd1-e1-h4, f4-f5, Bc1-h6 and Nf3-g5 and tries to bludgeon Black's king. The following game is a good example that I played recently.

☐ **G.Jones** ■ **D.Abhishek**
World Junior Championship, Yerevan 2007

1 e4 c5 2 Nc3 Nc6 3 Bb5 g6 4 Bxc6 dxc6 5 f4 Bg7 6 d3 Nf6 7 Nf3 0-0 8 0-0 b6 9 Qe1 Bg4 10 Ne5 Qc7 11 Qh4 Be6 12 Nf3 h6 13 f5 (Diagram 3)

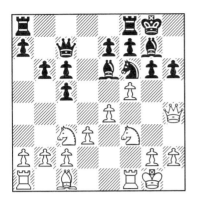

Diagram 3 (B)
White's standard pawn break

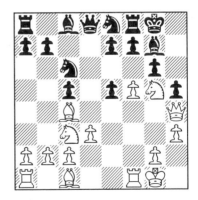

Diagram 4 (B)
Under heavy artillery fire

13...g5 14 Nxg5 hxg5 15 Bxg5 Bc8 16 Rf3 Rd8 17 Bh6 Ne8 18 Bxg7 Nxg7 19 Rh3 f6 20 Qh7+ Kf7 21 Qg6+ Kg8 22 Rf1 e6 23 Qh7+ Kf7 24 fxe6+ Bxe6 25 Rh6 Qe5 26 Qg6+ Kg8 27 Rxf6 (Diagram 4) 27...Qd4+ 28 Rf2 1-0

Below is another example of White's attack breaking straight through:

☐ B.Macieja ■ Joh.Alvarez
Bermuda 2001

---

1 e4 c5 2 Nc3 d6 3 f4 Nc6 4 Nf3 g6 5 Bc4 Bg7 6 0-0 Nf6 7 d3 0-0 8 Qe1 Bg4 9 e5 (Diagram 5)

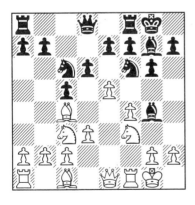

Diagram 5 (B)
The e-pawn goes first this time

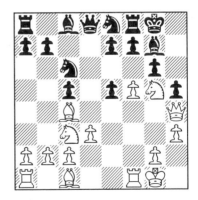

Diagram 6 (B)
And now the f-pawn follows

9

9...Ne8 10 Ng5 dxe5 11 Qh4 h5 12 h3 Bc8 13 f5 (Diagram 6) 13...Bxf5 14 Rxf5 Qd4+ 15 Qxd4 exd4 16 Rxf7 1-0

The following game illustrates the dangers for White if he attacks too early, before having enough pieces developed to follow the assault.

☐ **F.Hellers** ◼ **B.Gelfand**
Novi Sad Olympiad 1990

1 e4 c5 2 Nc3 d6 3 f4 Nc6 4 Nf3 g6 5 Bc4 Bg7 6 0-0 e6 7 f5?!

Too direct. 7 d3 Nge7 8 Qe1 is the main line which is analysed extensively in Chapter Three (2...d6).

7...exf5 8 d3 Nge7 9 Qe1 h6 10 exf5 Bxf5 (Diagram 7)

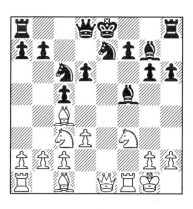

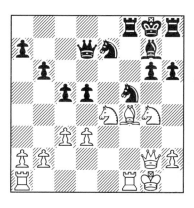

Diagram 7 (W)
White attacked too hastily

Diagram 8 (W)
Black is in control

Black has managed to win a pawn without his pawn structure having been damaged, and White is forced to weaken his own king to 'mix it up'.

11 g4!? Bxg4 12 Bxf7+ Kxf7 13 Ne5+ Kg8 14 Nxg4 Nd4

White has stopped Black castling but his own king is in fact weaker now, while the black knights start to dominate the position. To make matters worse, White hasn't even recaptured his pawn.

15 Qf2 Ndf5 16 Qg2 Qd7 17 Ne4 Rf8 18 c3 b6 19 Bf4 d5 (Diagram 8)

Black is in total control of the position.

20 Nd2 d4 21 Ne4 g5 22 Be5 Bxe5 23 Nxe5 Qe6 24 Ng4 dxc3 25 Rae1 Qc6 26 bxc3 Kg7 27 d4 Ng6 28 dxc5 bxc5 29 Qf2 Nd4 30 Nef6 h5 31 cxd4 hxg4 32 Ne8+ Qxe8! 0-1

The positional plan against Black's weakened queenside

In many lines of the Grand Prix Attack White forces structural weaknesses on the black queenside, normally by capturing the knight on c6 with his bishop and forcing Black to retake with the pawn. White can then try to target the weak c5-pawn with plans such as e4-e5, Nc3-a4 (or e4), b2-b3, Ba3 and perhaps c2-c4. The following game shows how White can continue piling the pressure on Black's weak pawns.

☐ I.Rogers ■ V.Johansson
Reykjavik 2006

1 e4 c5 2 Nc3 Nc6 3 Bb5 d6 4 Bxc6+ bxc6 5 f4 g6 6 Nf3 Bg7 7 0-0 Nf6 8 d3 0-0 9 Qe1 Rb8 10 b3 Ne8 11 Bd2 Nc7 12 Qh4 e6 13 Qxd8 Rxd8 14 e5 d5 15 Na4 Bf8 16 c4 (Diagram 9)

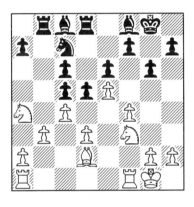

Diagram 9 (B)
Fixing the weakness on c5

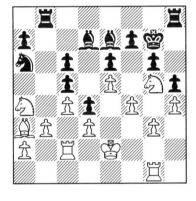

Diagram 10 (B)
The c5-pawn will fall

16...Na6 17 Ba5 Rd7 18 Rfd1 Nb4 19 Rd2 Kg7 20 g3 Bb7 21 Kf2 Be7 22 Ke2 h6 23 h4 h5 24 Rc1 Na6 25 Rb2 Bc8 26 Bd2 Rdb7 27 Be3 Rb4 28 Rcc2 d4 29 Bd2 R4b7 30 Rc1 Bd7 31 Rg1 Rh8 32 Bc1 Nc7 33 Rc2 Na6 34 Ba3 Rbb8 35 Ng5 (Diagram 10) 35...f5 36 exf6+ Bxf6 37 Nxc5 Nxc5 38 Bxc5 e5 39 Ne4 Rbe8 40 Kd2 Bg4 41 Nxf6 Kxf6 42 fxe5+ Ke6 43 Rf1 Bf5 44 Rf4 Rh7 45 Rxd4 Kxe5 46 Kc3 Kf6 47 Rd6+ Re6 48 Re2 Rxd6 49 Bxd6 Rd7 50 Be5+ Kf7 51 d4 1-0

In some lines, such as those in which Black plays an early ...e7-e6 and ...a7-a6, White has to change his plans slightly and play against Black's centre, trying to prove that it is a weakness. The following game is a good illustration of this theme.

☐ M.Lazic ■ K.Ninov
Novi Sad 1992

1 e4 c5 2 Nc3 Nc6 3 f4 e6 4 Nf3 a6 5 d3 d5 6 Qe2 Nf6 7 e5 Ng8 8 g3 Nh6 9 Bg2 Be7 10 0-0 d4 11 Ne4 Bd7 12 Bd2 Qb6 13 c4 0-0 14 Rab1 Rae8 15 Bh3 Nd8 16 b4 (Diagram 11)

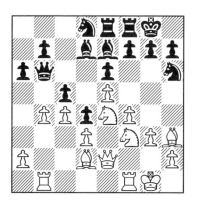

Diagram 11 (B)

Attacking on the queenside

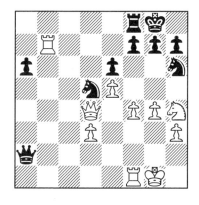

Diagram 12 (B)

White is winning

16...cxb4 17 c5 Bxc5 18 Nxc5 Qxc5 19 Bxb4 Qd5 20 Bg2 Bc6 21 Nh4 Qd7 22 Bxf8 Rxf8 23 Bxc6 Nxc6 24 h3 Ne7 25 g4 Nd5 26 Qe4 Qa4 27 Rxb7 Qxa2 28 Qxd4 (Diagram 12) 28...a5 29 g5 Qe2 30 Qf2 Qxf2+ 31 Rxf2 Nf5 32 Nxf5 exf5 33 Rb5 Nb4 34 d4 Rd8 35 d5 h6 36 g6 fxg6 37 Rd2 g5 38 d6 1-0

Black, on the other hand, plans to play on the queenside with ...b7-b5 and challenge in the centre with ...d7(d6)-d5. Black needs to be careful that he does not allow White's kingside attack to succeed and sometimes tries to play ...f7-f5 himself to stop White's breaks. After this, however, White can change his plan and target the weak squares that ...f7-f5 has created, such as e5 and g5.

I hope you enjoy this book and have many successes with the Grand Prix Attack.

Gawain Jones,
Enniskillen,
January 2008

Chapter One

2...Nc6 3 f4 g6 4 Nf3 Bg7 5 Bc4

▨ The First Few Moves

▨ Illustrative Games

▨ Conclusion

The First Few Moves

1 e4 c5 2 Nc3 Nc6 3 f4 g6 4 Nf3 Bg7 5 Bc4 (Diagram 1)

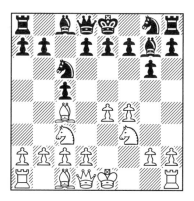
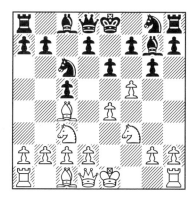

Diagram 1 (B)

White plays 5 Bc4

Diagram 2 (B)

White attacks straight away

In the next chapter we will examine the respectable alternative 5 Bb5, which is more fashionable and probably the sounder move. With 5 Bc4 White endeavours to destroy Black's defences straight away, but with correct play Black shouldn't have any problems. This is because he isn't yet committed to ...d7-d6 (see Chapter Three) and thus can play ...d7-d5 in one move, hitting the bishop. Nevertheless, against an unprepared opponent White can drum up a quick attack. A couple of years ago I got into deep trouble with Black in this line against someone much lower rated.

5...e6 6 f5 (Diagram 2)

The more restrained 6 0-0 is seen in Game 4.

6...Nge7

Lines where Black takes the pawn on f5 are covered in Game 1.

7 fxe6 fxe6

The alternative recapture, 7...dxe6, is examined in Game 2.

8 d3

8 0-0 0-0 9 d3 transposes to 8 d3 0-0 9 0-0 in the next note. If Black tries 8...d5 then 9 exd5 (9 Bb5 is unclear) 9...exd5 10 Nxd5!? Nxd5 11 Qe1+ is an interesting sacrifice. White has good practical play for the piece with the black king stuck in the centre of the board; e.g. 11...Nce7 12 Ng5 Qd7 13 a4 a6 14 d3 h6 15 Nf7 0-0 (15...Rf8! 16 Nxh6 Qd6 leaves White still to prove sufficient compensation) 16

Nxh6+ Bxh6 17 Bxh6 Rxf1+ 18 Qxf1 was unclear in M.Thesing-R.Lau, German League 1988.

8...d5

8...0-0 is also possible, intending to break with ...d7-d5 next move; i.e. 9 0-0 (or 9 Bg5 h6 10 Bh4 g5 11 Bf2 d5!?) 9...d5 10 Bb3 **(Diagram 3)** and then:

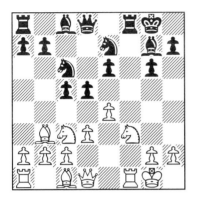

Diagram 3 (B)

The 8...0-0 variation

Diagram 4 (W)

Black takes over the queenside

a) 10...b5!? is still possible, even though White is able to take the pawn, as Black gets some compensation. For example, 11 Nxb5 Qb6 (or 11...c4) 12 Ba4 c4+ 13 Kh1 cxd3 14 cxd3 (14 Qxd3!?) 14...Ba6 15 exd5 Nxd5 16 Na3 Rad8 17 Nc4 Bxc4 18 dxc4 Nc3 19 Qb3 Nxa4 20 Qxa4 and White was slightly better in D.Rumens-O.Jackson, British Championship, Morecambe 1981.

b) 10...Nd4 11 Bg5 dxe4 (or 11...Nxb3 12 axb3 d4 13 Na4, since 13...b6? fails to 14 Bxe7 Qxe7 15 Nxb6) 12 Nxe4 h6 13 Bxe7 (rather than 13 Bd2 as in Art.Minasian-E.Ubilava, Protvino 1993) 13...Qxe7 14 c3 is also good for White.

c) 10...Na5 is more accurate, when 11 Bg5 d4! (11...Nxb3 transposes to the previous note) 12 Ne2 (12 Na4 is ineffective with the a-file still closed) 12...h6 13 Bd2 Nec6 14 Qe1 Nxb3 15 axb3 e5 was fine for Black in J.Ristoja-E.Inarkiev, European Club Cup, Izmir 2004.

d) 10...h6!? also comes into consideration.

9 Bb3 b5! (Diagram 4)

Black gains space on the queenside and White will have to make something of his initiative on the kingside in order not to be worse. This position is examined in Game 3.

Statistics

White's score is not brilliant in this line, but the average rating of the White players has been significantly lower than Black's. From 4312 games I found reaching the position after 5 Bc4, White has scored 42%, including 1316 wins and 2031 losses, with an average FIDE rating of 2137 compared to that of 2210 for the Black side. There have only been 29 recent games between players above 2300, but here White has managed 47% with 10 wins and 12 losses against a significantly stronger Black average.

Illustrative Games

Game 1
□ **Y.Meister** ■ **M.Manik**
Pardubice 1995

1 e4 c5 2 Nc3 Nc6 3 f4 g6 4 Nf3 Bg7 5 Bc4 e6

5...d6 would transpose to positions similar to 2...d6, but it's dubious as Black loses a tempo in his attempt to play ...d5. We will look at this variation in Chapter Three.

6 f5 gxf5 (Diagram 5)

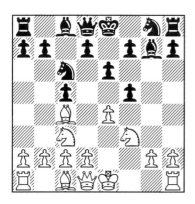

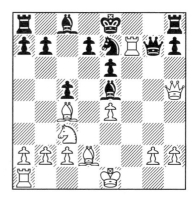

Diagram 5 (W)	Diagram 6 (B)
Black accepts the pawn	Coming, ready or not

After the alternative capture 6...exf5?! 7 exf5 gxf5 8 0-0 Black has no king cover and a terrible pawn structure. But more commonly he just ignores the white f5-

pawn, preferring to continue his own set-up with 6...Nge7. This is examined in the next two games.

7 d3!

7 exf5 d5 allows Black to construct an impressive centre. Therefore White declines to recapture the pawn, intent instead on quick development to try and exploit the weaknesses in Black's camp.

7...fxe4

This seems too risky. Better is 7...Nge7 8 0-0 d5 9 exd5 exd5. Then instead of 10 Bb3 as in P.Tishin-K.Kuderinov, Moscow 2005, I prefer 10 Bb5, after which White has very good play for the pawn; e.g. 10...0-0 11 Bxc6 Nxc6 12 Bg5 Qd6 13 Qd2 Nd4 14 Rae1 Nxf3+ 15 Rxf3 with an attack.

8 dxe4

Despite being a pawn down White has good prospects. He has a lead in development and open lines for his pieces, while Black's king is always going to be exposed. This miniature between two 2400-players shows White's ideas.

8...Ne5

After 8...Nge7 9 0-0 (9 Qd6!? Qa5 10 Bd2 Qb4 11 Qd3 is also worth considering) 9...Bxc3 10 bxc3 d5 11 Bb5 dxe4 12 Qxd8+ Kxd8 13 Ng5 Black's problems haven't been solved, despite the queen swap, and he can only watch as his extra pawns start dropping. *Fritz*'s suggestion of 8...Bxc3+ is hardly inspiring either: while it's true White's queenside pawn structure has been damaged, much more relevant is the weakening of the dark squares.

9 Nxe5 Bxe5 10 Qh5!

Gaining time on the bishop.

10...Qf6

10...d6 11 Bg5 Nf6 12 Qh4 leaves Black in an unpleasant pin.

11 Bd2 Ne7 12 Rf1! Qg7 13 Rxf7! (Diagram 6)

Sacrificing the exchange to weaken Black's position further. Notice the dark squares in particular, on which Black cannot counter White's attack.

13...Qxf7 14 Qxe5 0-0

This may seem an odd choice by Black as he has no pawn cover on the kingside, but it was just as risky to leave his king in the centre; e.g. 14...Rf8 15 0-0-0 a6 (if 15...b6 16 Nb5 wins at once) 16 Qxc5 b5 17 Bxb5! axb5 18 Nxb5 Ra6 19 Nc7+ Kd8 20 Nxa6 Bxa6 21 Qa5+, followed by 22 Qxa6 and wins.

15 0-0-0 (Diagram 7)

White has completed his development and can now direct all his pieces against the opposing king. Black, on the other hand, is still a long way from developing his queenside and, despite his material advantage, has less pieces participating.

Diagram 7 (B)
Black's queenside still slumbers

Diagram 8 (B)
The final sacrifice

15...b6 16 Bh6 Nc6

Black offers the exchange back to try and lessen the attack, but White correctly ignores it. Instead 16...Re8 allows White an immediate win with 17 Rf1 Qg6 18 Rf6! Qxg2 19 Rf3!!. The rook is invulnerable due to the mate on g7 and otherwise Rg3+ is coming next move.

17 Qd6! Re8 18 Rf1

Seizing the f-file.

18...Qe7

Forced, or else White mates on f8.

19 Qf4 Bb7 20 Nd5!! (Diagram 8)

Sacrificing another piece to enable his entire army to contribute to the attack.

20...exd5 21 exd5 1-0

White's threats are simply too strong. The knight on c6 is attacked, as well as the discovered check with d5-d6+, while after 21...Kh8 22 dxc6 Bxc6 23 Bg5! Black drops further material as he cannot counter both the threat to his queen and Bf6+ mating.

Game 2
□ **Alexa.Ivanov** ■ **M.Abeln**
Dutch Open Championship 1992

1 e4 c5 2 Nc3 Nc6 3 f4 g6 4 Nf3 Bg7 5 Bc4 e6 6 f5 Nge7 7 fxe6 dxe6

7...fxe6!? will be examined in the next game.

8 d3

8 0-0 will generally transpose as White plays d2-d3 next move; e.g. 8...0-0 9 d3 or 8...Nd4 9 d3.

8...0-0

Abeln actually played 8...Bd7 here and the game transposed after 9 0-0 0-0. However, Black can make an independent attempt to delay castling or even do without it entirely:

a) 8...Nd4 9 0-0 0-0 10 Bg5! is better for White, but 9...Nec6! is an alternative plan. Then after 10 Bg5 Nxf3+ (10...Qd7 11 Kh1 h6 12 Bh4 0-0 13 Nxd4 cxd4 14 Ne2 Ne5 15 Bb3 a5 16 a4 Ng4 17 Qd2 g5 18 Bf2 Kh7 19 Bg1 f5 was messy in S.Kecic-A.Delchev, Bled 1997) 11 Qxf3 Bd4+ (not 11...Qxg5? 12 Qxf7+) 12 Be3 Bxe3+ 13 Qxe3 Qd4 14 Qxd4 cxd4 15 Nb5 Ke7 equalized in G.Antoms-L.McShane, European Team Championship, Leon 2001. White should probably prefer 10 Be3 0-0 11 Nb5! when he has a slight advantage.

b) 8...h6!? **(Diagram 9)** is a novelty of Atalik's.

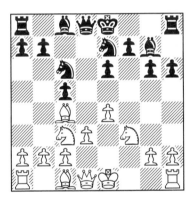

Diagram 9 (W)

Black plays 8...h6!?

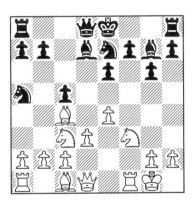

Diagram 10 (W)

Black plays 9...Na5

Black does not let White carry out his plan of 0-0, Qe1-h4 and tries for counterplay on the kingside rather than the more usual queenside play. S.Savchenko-S.Atalik, Bucharest 1996, continued 9 0-0 g5 10 Ne2 (10 Be3 is a slight improvement, and if 10...Nd4 11 Nb5!, while 10...b6 11 Qe1 gives White a comfortable advantage) 10...g4 11 Ne1 Ng6 12 Be3?! (White has no reason to sacrifice the b-pawn and could retain a slight edge with 12 c3) 12...Bxb2 13 Rb1 (13 Bxc5!? is unclear) 13...Bd4 14 Nxd4 cxd4 15 Bd2 and White had compensation for the pawn.

9 0-0 Bd7

M.Young-G.Jones, European Union Championship, Cork 2005, was the game I referred to in the introduction. Here I played 9...a6 10 a4 Bd7 11 Bg5 Na5 12 Qe1 Nxc4 13 dxc4 h6? (13...f6 14 Be3 is the lesser evil, though White is still on top) and was in a lot of trouble after 14 Qh4!, although I later managed to win.

Instead, 9...Na5 **(Diagram 10)** at once is the usual move, when White has two possibilities:

a) 10 Bb3 Nec6 11 Bg5 (or 11 Be3 Nxb3 12 axb3 b6 13 Qd2, and if 13...e5 14 Bh6 Be6 15 Bxg7 Kxg7 then 16 Ng5! Bc8 17 Rf2 f6 18 Raf1 with a slight advantage) 11...f6 12 Be3 Nxb3 (if 12...Nd4!? 13 e5!? fxe5 14 Ne4 White has a lot of compensation given Black's cramped bishops and bad pawn structure) 13 axb3 Nd4 (if 13...b6 14 d4!) 14 Na4 was slightly better for White in M.Pavlovic-S.Semkov, Yerevan 1988, or he might try 14 e5!? again.

b) 10 Qe1!? Nxc4 11 dxc4 and the doubled c-pawns, rather than being a weakness, control the centre. White threatens to play e4-e5 when he has a nice outpost on d6 for his knight; if Black prevents this by playing ...e6-e5 himself then White will have the d5 outpost. Black may do better just to continue with 10...Nec6!? as in the previous variation.

10 Qe1! (Diagram 11)

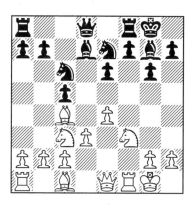

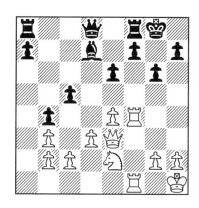

Diagram 11 (B)	Diagram 12 (B)
White has an easy game	Black is strategically lost

White has an easy position to play. Without the ...d7-d5 break Black struggles for counterplay, whereas White can either target the weak c5-pawn or play Qh4, Bh6 and Ng5 generating a quick attack.

10...Nd4

Now 10...Na5 is clearly better for White after 11 e5! Nxc4 12 dxc4, followed by Ne4 and Bg5 targeting the f6-square.

11 Nxd4 Bxd4+ 12 Kh1 Nc6 13 Bf4

13 Bh6 also gives White a comfortable advantage.

13...Be5 14 Qe3 Bxf4 15 Rxf4 Nd4 16 Raf1

Continuing to mount the pressure against f7.

16...b5

If 16...Nxc2 17 Qxc5 with a clear advantage.

17 Bb3 b4?!

17...a5 is a better try, as after 18 a3 Nxb3 19 cxb3 Black has an improved version of the game, though White still has a big advantage.

18 Ne2 Nxb3 19 axb3 (Diagram 12)

Black is strategically lost. He has no control over the dark squares and his c5- and f7-pawns are very weak. Furthermore, Black's king is exposed without the dark-squared bishop. As we will see, White's plan is very simple and Black is unable to stop it.

19...e5

19...f5 is *Fritz's* drastic suggestion, but after 20 exf5 exf5 21 Qxc5 White is a pawn up and still has the initiative.

20 Rf6! Qc7 21 Qh6 Rae8 22 Ng3 Re6 23 Nh5!

Forcing mate in eight.

23...gxh5 24 Qg5+ Kh8 25 Rxf7 1-0

Mate follows after 25...Rxf7 26 Rxf7 Rg6 27 Qxh5 Rg7 28 Rf8+ Rg8 29 Qf7! or 25...Rg8 26 Rxh7+! Kxh7 27 Rf7+ Kh8 28 Qxh5+.

Game 3
☐ W.Paschall ■ T.Bakre
Budapest 2001

---

1 e4 c5 2 Nc3 g6

Black uses a different move order, but it just transposes.

3 f4 Bg7 4 Nf3 Nc6 5 Bc4 e6 6 f5 Nge7 7 fxe6 fxe6 8 d3 d5

The point of 7...fxe6 and a problem with the 5 Bc4 line for White. Black takes the centre, gaining a tempo on the white bishop. The temporizing 8...0-0 was considered in the introduction to this chapter.

9 Bb3 b5! (Diagram 13)

Black threatens ...c5-c4 trapping the bishop; White cannot play 10 Nxb5 this time as Black has 10...Qa5+ 11 Nc3 d4 winning the white knight. Instead, 9...0-0 10 0-0 returns to 8...0-0 variations.

10 0-0

White sacrifices a piece in return for an attack and a couple of pawns. Instead:

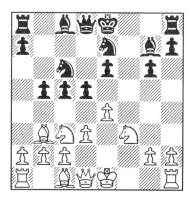

Diagram 13 (W)	**Diagram 14 (B)**
Black threatens ...c5-c4	White has good compensation

a) 10 a3 preserves the bishop but allows Black to equalize comfortably after 10...c4! 11 Ba2 a6 12 0-0 0-0 13 Bg5 Rf7 14 Qd2 Bb7, as in Art.Minasian-S.Tiviakov, Kherson 1991. More risky is 10...Nd4!? 11 Nxd4 cxd4 12 Ne2 dxe4 13 dxe4 0-0 14 Nf4 Kh8 15 0-0! (15 Bxe6? fails to 15...Rxf4!, while 15 Nxe6 Bxe6 16 Bxe6 Qb6 gives Black good compensation with White's king stuck in the middle) 15...Qb6 16 Nd3 Bb7 17 Bg5! and White was better in Art.Minasian-M.Khachian, Armenia 1992. Minasian seems to be the only GM who consistently plays this line of the Grand Prix.

b) 10 exd5 exd5 11 0-0 (not 11 Nxb5? Qa5+ 12 Nc3 c4! 13 dxc4 d4 and Black wins a piece) 11...c4! is a worse version of the game as Black can utilize the d5-square; for example, 12 dxc4 dxc4 13 Qxd8+ Nxd8! (13...Kxd8 14 Rd1+ is less clear) 14 Nxb5 cxb3 15 Nc7+ Kd7 16 Nxa8 bxc2 17 Rf2 Bb7, and now 18 Rd2+? is pointless in view of 18...Nd5, while 18 Rxc2 Bxa8 is better for Black with his two minor pieces.

10...c4

10...a6 also looks sensible for Black, simply maintaining his queenside pressure; e.g. 11 a3 0-0 and Black has at least equalized, S.Pizzuto-M.Petrillo, correspondence 1995. 10...Qb6 is suggested in Plaskett's *Sicilian Grand Prix Attack* and again Black is doing well after 11 exd5 c4+ 12 Kh1 cxb3 13 dxc6 bxc2 14 Qxc2 0-0. Black is no worse with his two bishops, despite *Fritz* preferring White.

11 dxc4 dxc4

Alternatively, Black can decline the piece and keep his central pawn mass: 11...bxc4 12 Ba4 Qb6+ 13 Kh1 d4 14 Bxc6+ Nxc6 15 Na4 Qa5 16 c3 d3?! (16...0-0 is better, as 17 cxd4 can be met by 17...Nxd4) 17 Ng5 Ne5 18 b4! Qd8 19 Nc5 Qe7 (and here 19...Qd6!? to prevent White's forthcoming queen manoeuvre) 20 Qa4+ Bd7 21 Qa6 Bc8 22 Qb5+ Bd7 23 Qb7 and White won in Gy.Horvath-A.Bokros, Hungarian Team Championship 1997.

12 Qxd8+

White swaps queens despite losing the b3-bishop, as he will get two pawns for the piece and a lead in development, while Black's pieces are badly coordinated.

12...Nxd8?!

This time 12...Kxd8 is preferable, although after 13 Nxb5 cxb3 14 axb3! **(Diagram 14)** White has good compensation for the piece with open files and good attacking chances. J.Ristoja-T.Franssila, Finnish Team Championship 2004, continued 14...Bd7, when Rogozenko suggests 15 Ng5 Kc8 16 c3!?.

The immediate 14 Ng5 allows simply 14...bxc2 (or 14...Nd4!? 15 Rd1 bxc2 16 Rd3 Nec6 17 e5 Ba6 18 Nxe6+ Ke7 19 Nexd4 Nxd4 20 Bg5+ Kf8 21 Rf1+ Kg8 22 Rxd4 Bxb5 and White had nothing, O.Hassan-J.Nilssen, Copenhagen 2001) 15 Nf7+ Kd7 16 Rf2 Nd4 17 Nxh8 Nxb5 and Black won in Z.Topel-K.Kisonova, World Junior Championships, Athens 2001.

13 Nxb5 cxb3 14 Nc7+ Kd7 15 Nxa8 bxc2 (Diagram 15)

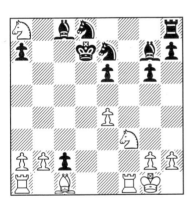

Diagram 15 (W)	Diagram 16 (B)
An intriguing position	White is a pawn up

An intriguing position has arisen where White is the exchange up but his knight on a8 is trapped and will ultimately fall, so he needs to see how much material he can win in the meantime. It is similar to the 10 exd5 exd5 11 0-0 c4! variation seen earlier, except that the e-pawns remain on the board.

 WARNING: Black should not rush to pick up the a8-knight with 15...Bb7? since 16 axb3 Bxa8 17 Rxa7+ would be clearly better for White.

16 Rf2

16 Bf4, trying to help the knight escape, fails to 16...Ndc6 17 Nc7 e5.

16...Bb7 17 Rd2+!

White gains time checking the black king. The immediate 17 Rxc2 Bxa8 18 Bf4 Ndc6 (18...Bxe4!?) 19 Rd1+ Ke8 was less testing for Black in Al.Andres Gonzalez-A.Garcia Luque, Spanish Team Championship 1995.

17...Kc8

Not 17...Ke8? 18 Nc7+ and the knight escapes.

18 Rxc2+ Ndc6?!

This leaves the knight vulnerable on e7. Black should prefer 18...Nec6 and then:

a) 19 Bg5 Bxa8 20 Rac1 Kb8 (not 20...Kc7? 21 b4 Kb6 22 a4 Nxb4 23 Be3+ Ka5 24 Rc7 and White recouped a piece in O.Biti-I.Jelen, Zagreb 1997) 21 Bxd8 Rxd8 22 Rxc6 Bxb2 ½-½ T.Karlsson-G.Sax, Stockholm 1999.

b) 19 Be3!? Kb8 (or 19...Bxa8 20 Bxa7) 20 Nb6 axb6 21 Bxb6 Nf7 22 Rd1 Nfe5 23 Ng5 Bc8 24 a3 was C.Bouzoukis-A.Wojtkiewicz, Washington DC 1997. White's rook and connected passed pawns work better than Black's two pieces in this position.

19 Bg5!

Threatening to take on e7 due to the pin down the c-file, while if 19...Kb8 20 Nc7! and the knight is invulnerable.

19...Re8 20 Rac1 Bxa8

20...Kd7? 21 Rd1+ Kc8 doesn't help, since apart from 22 Rd6 Bxa8 23 Bxe7 Rxe7 24 Rdxc6+ Bxc6 25 Rxc6+ transposing to the game, White can go for more with 22 b4!.

21 Bxe7 Rxe7 22 Rxc6+ Bxc6 23 Rxc6+ (Diagram 16)

White is now a pawn up in the ending which he eventually converted.

23...Kb7

23...Kd7 24 Ra6 Ke8 25 b3 Bh6 26 Kf2 also led to a win for White in L.Gomez Cabrero-R.Sheldon, World Junior Championships, Oropesa del Mar 1998.

24 Rc2 Bh6 25 Kf2 Rd7 26 Ke2 Rd6 27 b3 Rd7 28 Rc4 a5 29 e5 Bg7 30 Rc5 Kb6 31 Rc8 Rd5 32 Re8 Bxe5 33 Rxe6+ Bd6 34 Nd2 Kc7 35 h3 Bb4 36 Nc4 Rg5 37 g4 Kd7 38 Ra6 Ke8 39 Kf3 Kf8 40 Ra8+ Kg7 41 Ra7+ Kg8 42 a3 Bc3 43 a4 Bb4 44 Rd7 h5 45 Ne3 hxg4+ 46 hxg4 Rc5 47 Nd5 Be1 48 Ke4 Rc2 49 Ke5 Rg2 50 Ke6 Bh4 51 Ra7 Re2+ 52 Kd6 Bg3+ 53 Kd7 Rb2 54 Rxa5 Rxb3 55 Ke6 Kg7 56 Rb5 Ra3 57 Rb4 Kh6 58 Re4 Kg5 59 Kd7 Ra1 60 Rc4 Be1 61 Kc6 Rb1 62 Nc7 Kh4 63 Ne6 g5 64 Ng7 Kg3 65 Kd5 Bd2 66 Ke6 Rf1 67 Nf5+ Kh3 68 Rd4 Re1+ 69 Kf7 Bf4 70 Nh6 Ra1 71 Kg6 Kh4 72 Nf7 Kxg4 73 Nxg5 Kg3 74 Ne6 Be3 75 Rc4 Kf3 76 Kf5 Bd2? 77 Nd4+ Kg3 78 Nb3 Rf1+ 79 Ke5 Bf4+ 80 Kd5 Rd1+ 81 Kc6 Kg4 82 a5 Kf5 83 a6 Be3 84 Nc5 Ra1 85 Ra4 Rc1 86 Ra5 Kf6 87 a7 Bxc5 88 Rxc5 Ra1 89 Kb7 Rb1+ 90 Ka6 1-0

Game 4
☐ G.Giorgadze ■ J.Corral Blanco
Spanish Team Championship 2003

1 e4 c5 2 Nc3 Nc6 3 f4 g6 4 Nf3 Bg7 5 Bc4 e6 6 0-0

Rather than hitting with f4-f5 straight away, White simply completes his development.

6...Nge7 7 d3

7 e5 fails to gain White any advantage after 7...d6; e.g. 8 exd6 Qxd6 9 d3 0-0 10 Ne4 Qc7 11 Qe1 Nf5 12 Qf2 b6 and Black was fine in J.Polgar-B.Gelfand, Pacs (rapid) 2003.

7...d5 8 Bb3 0-0 9 Qe1 (Diagram 17)

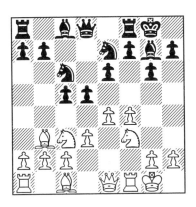

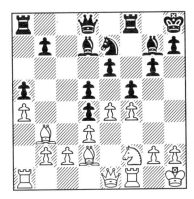

Diagram 17 (B)	Diagram 18 (B)
Position after 9 Qe1	White plans Nh3-g1-f3

NOTE: White continues in classic Grand Prix Attack style, but this should not give him much advantage here as Black has succeeded in playing ...d5 in one go (i.e. ...d7-d5 rather than ...d7-d6 first and then ...d6-d5).

However, Giorgi Giorgadze is a strong grandmaster and he's played this position several times, so he must believe in it for White.

9...Nd4

9...Na5!? is another option.

10 Nxd4 cxd4 11 Nd1 a5 12 a4 f5

Black tries to block up the kingside and halt the white attack, while White just continues developing his pieces.

25

12...dxe4 was played in another Giorgadze game: after 13 dxe4 b6 14 Rf3! (an interesting new idea – White tries to attack down the h-file with a quick 'rook lift'; the old move was 14 Nf2) 14...Ba6 15 Rh3 Nc6 (15...Rc8!?) 16 Nf2 Qe7 17 e5 White had the advantage in G.Giorgadze-Gil.Hernandez, Spanish Team Championship 2002.

13 Nf2 Bd7 14 Bd2 Kh8 15 Kh1!? (Diagram 18)

Moving the king to a safer square. It is unlikely that White will want to play a move such as g2-g4 continuing the attack. Instead he can now use the g1-square for his knight (i.e. Nf2-h3-g1), which can then go on to f3 and look to jump either to g5 or to the outpost on e5.

 TIP: Remember, when you cannot find a clear plan, try to improve the position of your worst placed piece.

15...Bc6

Black stops the white knight from moving just yet as it is required to defend e4.

16 exf5! Nxf5

16...exf5 17 Nh3 gives White a clear advantage. He has the nice outpost on e5 for his knight, whereas the corresponding square of e4 for the black knight cannot be used due to the pawn on d3, while Black's bishops are blocked in by his own pawns.

17 Ng4!

The knight looks to go into the e5 outpost. The greedy 17 Qxe6? would be a blunder due to 17...Re8 18 Qf7 Re7 and the white queen is embarrassed for squares.

17...Qb6 18 Rf3!?

Defending the e3-square again to try to stop Black's knight from jumping in where it would be a nuisance, while also planning the rook lift that we saw in Giorgadze's earlier game.

18...Qc5 19 Rh3

Indirectly attacking e6, as now after White takes on e6, the g6-pawn will be attacked due to the pin along the file.

19...Bd7 20 Ne5!

Hitting the bishop and threatening Nxg6+.

20...Be8

Black is horribly passive and his king is very weak, while White's pieces continue to manoeuvre to their best squares.

21 Nf3! (Diagram 19)

Knight retreats are always hard to spot. White attacks the e6-pawn with his queen and threatens to play Ng5, attacking both e6 and h7.

1...Bf6

If 21...Bd7 22 Ng5 h6 23 Nxe6 wins, so Black decides to give up the e6-pawn at once.

22 Qxe6 Bc6 23 Ne5

But now White is a pawn up and still has a strong attack.

23...Bxe5 24 Qxg6!

Instead of recapturing the bishop straight away White takes the g6-pawn, threatening mate. Black cannot both stop the mate and retreat his bishop.

24...Qe7 25 fxe5 Ne3 26 Qd6 Qxd6 27 exd6 Rf2 28 Bxe3 dxe3 29 Rxe3

Black has halted the attack and exchanged queens, while his pieces are starting to look active. Unfortunately, it has cost him three pawns, so White has a technically winning position.

29...Raf8 30 Kg1 d4 31 Rg3 R2f6 32 Re1 Rxd6 33 Re7 Rg6 34 Rxg6 hxg6 35 Re5 Ra8 (Diagram 20)

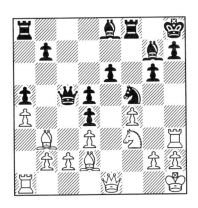

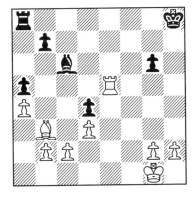

Diagram 19 (B)

An attacking retreat

Diagram 20 (W)

White wins easily

Black has recouped one pawn, but White still has two extra and has regained the initiative. The rest is easy.

36 Re6 Kg7 37 Rd6 Re8 38 Rxd4 Re2 39 Rg4 Re1+ 40 Kf2 Rb1 41 Rg5 Rxb2 42 Rxa5 Kf6 43 Rc5 Ke7 44 a5 Kd6 45 Rg5 Be8 46 Rd5+ Kc7 47 Re5 Bd7 48 Re1!

The simplest way to win. White keeps the black rook trapped on b2 from where it cannot escape.

48...Bc6 49 Ke3 1-0

White's plan of Kd2-c3 winning the trapped rook cannot be prevented.

Conclusion

5 Bc4 is an interesting line which can be used as a good surprise weapon, but objectively it should not trouble Black. The critical line is undoubtedly that seen in Game 3 (Paschall-Bakre) where Black can either win the piece (as in the game), which leaves the position extremely messy, or else try one of the alternatives such as 10...a6. In these lines White is in very real danger of being worse. The straightforward 6 0-0 of Game 4 is a quieter way of playing for White, where he simply develops his pieces and does not try for much of an advantage, hoping instead for a position he understands better than his opponent.

Chapter Two

2...Nc6 3 f4 g6 4 Nf3 Bg7 5 Bb5

■ The First Few Moves

■ Illustrative Games

■ Conclusion

The First Few Moves

1 e4 c5 2 Nc3 Nc6 3 f4 g6

3...e6 transposes to 2...e6 3 f4 Nc6, which is examined in Chapter Four.

4 Nf3 Bg7

After 4...d6 I advocate 5 Bc4, reaching positions in the next chapter (2...d6 3 f4), as 5 Bb5 Bd7 6 d3 Bg7 7 0-0 a6! is fine for Black.

5 Bb5 (Diagram 1)

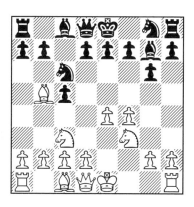

Diagram 1 (B)	**Diagram 2 (W)**
White plays 5 Bb5	Black's usual response

The main line of the whole Grand Prix Attack. Instead of 5 Bc4, seen in the previous chapter, White opts for the more positional 5 Bb5. As White's light-squared bishop often gets into trouble in the 5 Bc4 lines, he tries to get rid of the troublesome piece and, if possible, double the black queenside pawns. As well as damaging Black's structure, it also makes it harder for him to drum up any counterplay. This is the most theoretical line of the Grand Prix Attack, but there still isn't that much theory to know.

5...Nd4 (Diagram 2)

Black's choice in 80% of games. Other moves reach positions similar to Chapter Six (2 Nc3 Nc6 3 Bb5) as White follows up with Bxc6. For instance, 5...d6 6 Bxc6+ bxc6 transposes to Game 27 (Hernandez-Minzer), and 5...Nh6 6 Bxc6 bxc6 is Game 28 (Jones-Stojanovski). Instead, 5...e6 leaves holes on the dark squares after 6 Bxc6 and 7 e5, while 5...a6 just wastes a move as White was planning to take on c6 anyway.

6 0-0

The main move, but White has several other options:

a) 6 a4 has been played by Michael Adams, England's top grandmaster, though not with particularly good results. For example, 6...e6 (6...a6 7 Bd3!? can be compared with 6 Bd3!? below) 7 0-0 (7 e5!? a6 8 Bc4 d5! 9 exd6 Nh6 is equal) 7...Ne7 8 e5 a6 9 Bd3 (9 Be2!? is worth considering, with the possible line 9...d5! 10 Nxd4 cxd4 11 Nb1 g5!?) Nxf3+ 10 Qxf3 d5! and Black is doing well as he controls the centre, M.Adams-I.Morovic Fernandez, Las Palmas 1993.

b) 6 Nxd4 was played by the top Russian GM Morozevich, but it seems an inferior version of a line from Chapter Seven: 3 Bb5 Nd4 4 Bc4 g6 5 Nf3 Bg7 6 Nxd4 cxd4 7 Qf3 (see Game 36). Here White has played f2-f4 (rather than Bb5-c4) and so doesn't have any tricks against f7. Nevertheless Morozevich found a way to retain some advantage after 6...cxd4 7 Ne2 a6 8 Ba4 b5 9 Bb3 e6 10 0-0 Ne7 11 d3 0-0 12 Qe1 f5 13 Bd2 Nc6 14 Kh1 Bb7 15 Ng1! h6 16 Nf3 in A.Morozevich-M.Adams, Tilburg 1993. Instead, 7...Qb6 is suggested by Rogozenko and seems to give Black a fine game, such as after 8 Bd3 d5! 9 e5 f6.

c) 6 Bc4!? is again comparable to Chapter Seven (3 Bb5 Nd4 4 Bc4), although White usually dispenses with f2-f4 in that line. E.Sutovsky-S.Tiviakov, Bled Olympiad 2002, continued 6...d6 7 0-0 e6 8 e5!? Nxf3+ 9 Qxf3 d5 10 Bb5+ Bd7 11 Bxd7+ Qxd7 12 d4! cxd4 13 Ne2 Ne7 14 Nxd4 and White was slightly better.

d) 6 Bd3!? has been tried by Judit Polgar, the strongest female player in history, and will be examined in Game 12.

e) 6 Ba4?! is inferior after 6...Qa5! 7 Bb3 b5 (or 7...Nxb3 8 cxb3 d6) 8 Nxd4 cxd4 9 Nb1 Bb7 10 Qe2 Nf6 11 e5 Ne4 12 Na3 a6 13 0-0 Nc5 and Black had good play in B.Damljanovic-Z.Ribli, Reggio Emilia 1988/89.

6...Nxb5

The main line, examined in the first four games of this chapter. Other options are covered in Game 9 (6...e6) and Games 10-11 (6...a6).

7 Nxb5 d5!? (Diagram 3)

Black's most testing response, though he can also play 7...d6 (see Games 7 and 8). 7...a6 does not have much independent significance. For instance, 8 Nc3 d6 9 d4 cxd4 10 Nxd4 is the note to Black's 9th move in Game 7, while 9 d3 Nf6 10 Qe1 is a standard Grand Prix Attack similar to that in Game 8.

8 exd5

The main alternative 8 e5!? is seen in Game 6. 8 d3 is also possible but does not guarantee White an advantage: 8...a6 9 Nc3 Bxc3 10 bxc3 dxe4 11 dxe4 Qxd1 12 Rxd1 Nf6 was fine for Black in A.Kosten-A.Shirov, Val Maubuee 1989.

8...a6!

8...Nf6?! would allow White to support the pawn with 9 c4, while 8...Qxd5?? of course loses to 9 Nc7+.

9 Nc3 Nf6 10 d4 (Diagram 4)

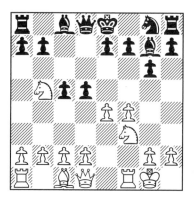

Diagram 3 (W)
Black counters in the centre

Diagram 4 (B)
The critical position

The critical position in the Grand Prix Attack. If Black can recapture the pawn on d5 without harm he will be doing well with his two bishops, so White has to make the best possible use of his initiative. This is examined in the first game below (Benjamin-Smith).

Statistics

In the 3329 games I have with this line White has scored just over 50% against a slightly higher average rating (2197 for White, compared to 2234 for Black); White has a slight plus with 1199 wins to Black's 1184. For the games from the last few years between players rated above 2300, White has scored 51% with 17 wins and 16 losses, also against a slightly higher average rating.

Illustrative Games

Game 5
□ **J.Benjamin** ■ **B.Smith**
Philadelphia World Open 2006

1 e4 c5 2 Nc3 g6 3 f4 Bg7 4 Nf3 Nc6 5 Bb5 Nd4 6 0-0 Nxb5 7 Nxb5 d5 8 exd5
White's other main option is 8 e5!?, which is the subject of the next game.
8...a6 9 Nc3

9 Na3!? is an interesting alternative: 9...Qxd5 10 d3 Nh6 (10...b5 11 c4!?) 11 Nc4 Qd8 12 a4 Be6 13 Ne3 0-0 14 a5 and White was for preference in J.M.Degraeve-M.Senff, Metz 2001.

9...Nf6

9...Bd4+?! is an unusual attempt to halt White's plan of d2-d4, but it didn't work well in the following game: 10 Kh1 (10 Nxd4 cxd4 11 Ne4 Qxd5 is unclear) 10...Nf6 (on 10...Bg4 Bangiev gives 11 h3 Bxf3 12 Qxf3 Nf6 13 Ne2!, when 13...Qxd5? loses the bishop to 14 c3, while 13...Nxd5 14 Nxd4 cxd4 15 c4! promises White a clear advantage) 11 Ne2! Nxd5 12 Nexd4 cxd4 13 Nxd4 and White was just a pawn up in L.Christiansen-E.Lobron, Essen 1999.

10 d4 Nxd5

Black has two other choices:

a) 10...cxd4 is hardly ever played, though it's not as bad as it seems. After 11 Qxd4 0-0 12 Ne5 (if 12 Be3 Ng4) 12...Bf5 (B.Lach-M.Bauer, German League 1996) Black has compensation for the pawn, but White should still retain some advantage.

b) 10...c4 **(Diagram 5)** is probably Black's safest option, trying to keep the centre closed while he recaptures the d5-pawn, and then:

Diagram 5 (W)	Diagram 6 (B)
Black's safest option	Theoretically important

b1) 11 Ne5 Nxd5 12 Qf3 (12 Nxc4?! Nxc3 13 bxc3 Qc7 is better for Black according to Hodgson) 12...e6. Plaskett considers this position unclear, while Rowson thinks that, while Black is comfortable, there is still a lot of play and White is not worse. Personally I would prefer playing White as he has the initiative. J.Hodgson-J.Rowson, 4th matchgame, Rotherham 1997, continued 13 f5 (Rowson suggests 13 a4!?, 13 Ne4!? and 13 b3!? as possible alternatives) 13...gxf5 14 Nxd5 (or 14 Qg3 Rg8 15 Bh6 Kf8 and Black is at least okay, though he will have to defend carefully for a few moves) 14...Qxd5 15 Qxd5 exd5 16 Nf3 0-0 and the game was drawn on move 29.

b2) 11 Qe2!? b5 12 Re1 (Rowson also offers the interesting 12 Bd2!? Nxd5 13 Nxd5 Qxd5 14 Bb4, when Black will find it slightly tricky to complete his development without dropping the e-pawn) 12...Bb7 13 f5! Nxd5 14 Bg5 0-0 15 Nxd5 Qxd5 16 Bxe7 Rfe8 17 fxg6 hxg6 18 Qf2 is the line given in *Chess Openings for White Explained*. White has an extra pawn and Black's compensation with the two bishops should not be enough here.

11 dxc5!

11 Nxd5 Qxd5 12 dxc5 Qxc5+ 13 Kh1 0-0 gave White nothing in A.Bennett-R.Dzindzichashvili, New York Open 1993, whereas Black had the two bishops.

11...Nxc3 12 Qxd8+ Kxd8 13 bxc3 (Diagram 6)

An interesting position and one of great importance to this variation of the Grand Prix Attack. White's pawn structure has been shattered and Black has the two bishops, but it is not as straightforward as it seems: Black's king is exposed on d8 and White has the open d-file and semi-open b-file for his rooks and a good square on e5 for his knight, while b6 is a clear weakness in Black's camp. I prefer White here as it is difficult for Black to unwind.

13...Bxc3 14 Rb1 Kc7 15 Rb3!

Forcing the bishop to relinquish the a5-e1 diagonal so that White can use it for his own bishop.

15...Bf6 16 Bd2

Eyeing up the a5-square.

16...Be6

16...a5 might be better, stopping White's plan, but he has at least a slight advantage after 17 Rfb1, keeping the pressure on Black.

17 Ba5+ Kc6

17...Kc8 18 Rb6 Bxa2 19 Ne5 gives White very good compensation for the pawn as Black is nowhere near developing his rooks.

18 Rb6+ Kxc5 19 Nd2! (Diagram 7)

Starting to set up a mating net. Black is a pawn up but cannot cope with all White's pieces around his king.

19...Bd5 20 c4! Bc6

20...Bxc4 21 Rc1 Bd4+ 22 Kh1 Be3 does not save Black, as 23 Rxc4+ Kd5 24 Rbb4 keeps the piece.

21 Rd1!

The mating net is almost complete.

21...Kd6

forced, as White was threatening mate in a few moves with Nb3+; e.g. 21...Rac8 22 Nb3+ Kxc4 23 Rb4+ Kc3 24 Rd2! and mates.

22 Ne4+ Ke6?!

22...Kc7 is a better try, although White is still winning after the following neat combination: 23 Rb2+ Kb8 24 Nxf6 exf6 25 Bb6! when Black is playing without his a8-rook and cannot stop White's plan of Rbd2 and Rd8; e.g. 25...Rc8 26 Rd6 (if 26 Rbd2 Ba4) 26...a5 27 Rbd2 Ra6 28 c5 followed by 29 Rd8 and wins.

23 g4!

Joel Benjamin continues his impeccable play, hounding the black king and using all his pieces in the mating attack. Black must now move the bishop to give his king a square.

23...Bh4 24 Nc5+ Kf6 25 Bc3+ e5 26 Rxc6+

Creating a picturesque winning position, although 26 Nxb7 Rhc8 27 Na5 is the most accurate, picking up the bishop on c6 and continuing the attack.

26...bxc6 27 Bxe5+ Ke7 28 Rd7+ Ke8 29 g5! (Diagram 8)

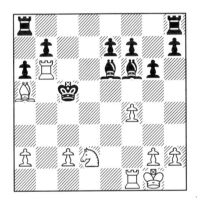 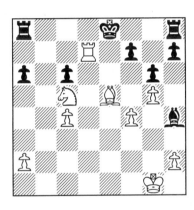

Diagram 7 (B)	Diagram 8 (B)
Setting up a mating net	Black's forces are scattered

29 Bxh8 Be7 is less clear. After the text all Black's pieces are out of the game. He would still be okay if he could play ...0-0, but unfortunately that is not a legal move.

29...Be1

After 29...Rg8 30 Bf6 White threatens to mate by 31 Re7+ Kd8 32 Nb7+ Kc8 33 Nd6+ Kb8 34 Rb7. Black's only defence is 30...Rb8, but this allows 31 Re7+ (the move humans would play, though 31 Rd2! is forced mate according to *Fritz*) 31...Kd8 32 Nxa6, when Black cannot keep his rook and White's attack continues

35

(if 32...Rb1+ 33 Re1+ or 32...Rc8 33 Rxf7+ Ke8 34 Re7+ Kd8 35 Nc5 wins).

30 Rb7 Bd2

30...Rg8 31 Bf6 is similar to the previous note.

31 Ne4 1-0

Black drops even more material; i.e. 31...Rd8 32 Bxh8 or if 31...Be3+ 32 Kg2 Rg8 33 Nd6+ mates.

Game 6
☐ **Art.Minasian** ■ **T.A.Petrosian**
Yerevan 2004

1 e4 c5 2 Nc3 Nc6 3 f4 g6 4 Nf3 Bg7 5 Bb5 Nd4 6 0-0 Nxb5 7 Nxb5 d5 8 e5!? (Diagram 9)

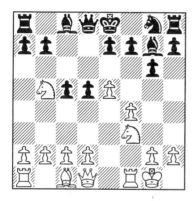 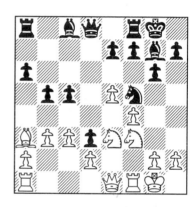

Diagram 9 (B)	**Diagram 10 (B)**
Keeping the centre closed	White has the advantage

White chooses to keep the centre closed and blocks the g7-bishop out of the game. This leads to more complex positions than the 8 exd5 lines. White intends to follow up with d2-d4 when he has a space advantage and more control over the centre, while Black's advantage of the two bishops is diminished as there are no open lines for them.

8...a6

The main move, forcing the knight to retreat immediately. Instead:

a) 8...d4 prevents d2-d4 but leaves White ahead in development after 9 c3 a6 10 Na3 and then:

a1) 10...d3 11 Nc4 (White brings his knight round to a more active post) 11...b5 12

Ne3 Nh6 13 b3 Nf5 14 Qe1 0-0 15 Ba3 **(Diagram 10)** is an extremely unusual position, but I think White holds some advantage. The pawn on d3 is more likely to be a weakness than a strength after White has repositioned his pieces. The c5-pawn is also awkward to defend and Black's pawn pushing has not helped his development. M.Hebden-O.Thorsson, Kopavogur 1994, continued 15...b4!? 16 cxb4 cxb4 17 Bxb4 Qb6 18 Bc3 Bb7 19 Qf2 Nxe3 20 Qxe3 Qxe3+ 21 dxe3 and White was a pawn up.

a2) 10...b5 11 cxd4 cxd4 12 Nc2!? d3 13 Ne3, Art.Minasian-Y.Pelletier, World Team Championship, Lucerne 1997, is similar to the previous note except without the c-pawns. I'm not sure who this favours, as although White can now develop his bishop to b2, he does not have the c5-pawn to target.

Instead of 12 Nc2!?, Bangiev suggests the sensible-looking 12 d3. His line runs 12...Nh6 (if 12...Bg4 13 Nc2 f6 14 h3 Bxf3 15 Qxf3 Rc8 16 Qf2 targets d4) 13 Nc2 Nf5 14 g4 Ne3!? 15 Bxe3 dxe3 16 Nxe3 h5 with compensation for Black, but I believe White is doing well after 17 g5 as the bishop on g7 will find it very difficult to perform any active role in the game, so White's advanced kingside pawns should not weaken him too much.

b) 8...Nh6 9 d4 a6 10 Nc3 c4, Art.Minasian-P.Froehlich, Linares 2001, is similar to the 10...c4 variation, examined as an alternative to 10...cxd4 below.

c) 8...b6!? is mentioned by Plaskett. I can only find one game with this move and both players were very lowly rated. I would think that 9 d4 Ba6 10 a4 would provide White with some advantage.

9 Nc3 Bg4

Now after 9...d4 the white knight can take up a more favourable post in the centre: 10 Ne4 Qd5 11 d3 Nh6 12 Qe1 0-0 13 a4 a5 14 Nfd2! b6 15 Nc4 and White was better in S.Iuldachev-D.Harika, Commonwealth Championship, Mumbai 2004.

10 d4 cxd4

Taking the pawn allows White some nice squares for his pieces, whereas the alternative 10...c4 **(Diagram 11)** leaves White with a big centre.

I have actually played this position a couple of times for Black and while my results are quite good, I believe this position to be better for White. For example, 11 h3 Bxf3 12 Qxf3 e6 13 g4!? (or 13 b3 Rc8 14 Ba3 h5, G.Quillan-G.Jones, Gibraltar 2007, and now perhaps 15 Rab1 would keep Black tied down) 13...Ne7 14 f5! (better than 14 Be3 h5 15 Bf2 Qd7 16 Nd1 0-0-0 17 Ne3 hxg4 18 hxg4 f5 as in B.Heberla-G.Jones, Calvia 2006) 14...gxf5 15 Bg5!. I remember I analysed this for some time and came to the conclusion that it is not a pleasant position for Black to defend.

11 Qxd4 e6 12 Ne1

Not allowing Black to swap off his light-squared bishop which now has a shortage of squares, and 13 h3 followed by 14 g4 threatens to trap it.

Instead 12 Qb4!? b5 13 Be3 Bf8 14 Bc5 Bxc5+ (14...Qb6!?) 15 Qxc5 Rc8 16 Qa7 Ra8 was fine for Black in O.Jackson-J.Gallagher, British Championship, Scarborough 1999. Alternatively, 12...Bxf3 13 Rxf3 b5! is unclear according to Hodgson, but not 13...Qe7? 14 Qa4+! Qd7 15 Qxd7+ Kxd7 16 Na4! which left Black in a lot of trouble in J.Hodgson-J.Rowson, 2nd matchgame, Rotherham 1997.

12...h5

Safeguarding the bishop.

13 Qf2! (Diagram 12)

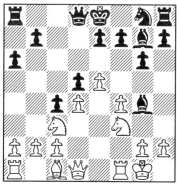

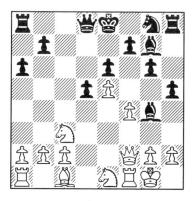

Diagram 11 (W)	Diagram 12 (B)
White has a big centre	White begins to regroup

White starts regrouping his pieces.

> **TIP: You do not want to blockade a pawn with your queen as it wastes her power, so it is normally advisable to try to block it with a knight instead. This usually means that the knight finds a nice outpost in front of the pawn as well.**

13...Ne7 14 h3 Bf5 15 Nf3!

Now that Black can no longer trade his bishop for it, the knight comes back again and eyes the d4-square. Furthermore, Black's bishop on f5 is looking rather stupid as that square is better suited for his knight.

15...Rc8 16 Be3 Qc7 17 Rac1

Defending c2, allowing White to move his c3-knight.

17...b5 18 a3 Nc6 19 Bb6!

19 Bc5? is not possible straight away due to 19...Nxe5 with a discovered attack on the bishop, so White first forces the black queen to move.

19...Qb7 20 Bc5 (Diagram 13)

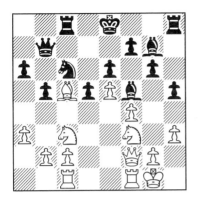

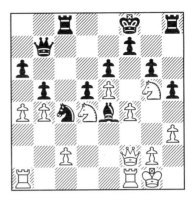

Diagram 13 (B)

Black has problems

Diagram 14 (B)

Breaking up the queenside

Black already has some problems. He cannot castle, his bishop on f5 is ineffectual, as is the one on g7, and it is hard for him to find an active plan. Meanwhile White controls the d4 and c5-squares, stopping Black's ...d5-d4 break, and thereby dominates in the centre.

20...Na5 21 Ne2

Continuing to regroup his pieces. The knight is now gazing at the juicy d4-square.

21...Qc6 22 b4!

Cementing the bishop on c5.

22...Nc4 23 Ned4 Qb7 24 Ra1 Be4 25 Ng5

White does not want Black to be able to swap his bishop for the knight and keeps him in a very cramped position.

25...Bf8 26 Bxf8 Kxf8 27 a4! (Diagram 14)

White breaks on the queenside, exploiting his more active pieces. Black is lost already. He cannot avoid losing at least a pawn on the queenside, while White still holds all the positional trumps of the position: the d4, c5 and g5-squares, the a-file, plus the fact that White has the only pawn-breaks so Black is forced to remain passive.

27...Ra8

If 27...bxa4 28 Rxa4 Kg7 29 Rfa1 Ra8, White wins with 30 b5! axb5 31 Ra7!! Rxa7 32 Rxa7 Qxa7 33 Ndxe6+ and 34 Qxa7+.

28 axb5 Kg7

28...axb5 29 Rxa8+ Qxa8 30 Nxb5 is also hopeless for Black.

29 bxa6 Qxb4 30 Rab1 Qd2 31 Rb7 Qxf2+ 32 Kxf2 Rhe8 33 a7 1-0

Game 7
☐ B.Macieja ■ P.Wells
European Championship, Warsaw 2005

1 e4 c5 2 Nc3 Nc6 3 f4 g6 4 Nf3 Bg7 5 Bb5 Nd4 6 0-0 Nxb5 7 Nxb5 d6 8 d4!? (Diagram 15)

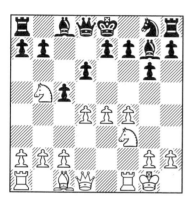

Diagram 15 (B)

White opens the centre

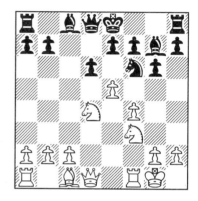

Diagram 16 (B)

The aggressive option

White opens the centre to try and exploit his lead in development. 8 d3 is examined in the next game. 8 a4 preventing ...b7-b5 is also possible, but it does cost White a move, which could be spent furthering his ambitions elsewhere.

8...cxd4

Instead:

a) 8...a6 9 Nc3 cxd4 10 Nxd4 has the appearance of a Sicilian Dragon. White has lost his light-squared bishop for a knight but has gained several tempi and is ready to launch a quick attack. Note that winning the b2-pawn with 10...Qb6 11 Be3 Qxb2 is far too greedy, as after 12 Nd5 Black cannot defend against the threats of both 13 Nc7+ and 13 Qd3 followed by 14 Rfb1 trapping the queen.

b) 8...Qb6 9 a4! a6 10 Nc3 cxd4 11 Nd5 (targeting the weak b6-square caused by ...a7-a6) 11...Qc5 (11...Qd8 12 a5 leaves White with a clear edge) 12 b4 Qa7 (if 12...Qc6? 13 b5! wins) 13 Qd3 and White is going to recapture the pawn on d4 soon, leaving Black with terribly uncoordinated pieces.

9 Nbxd4 Nf6 10 e5 (Diagram 16)

The aggressive and critical option. Otherwise the only way White can defend his e-pawn is with a move such as 10 Qd3, when he can perhaps claim a slight advantage due to his central control, but Black shouldn't be too unhappy with his two bishops and solid position.

10...Nd5

10...Ng4 is also possible, when White's best plan looks to be sacrificing the e5-pawn with 11 c3 dxe5 12 Nxe5 Nxe5 13 fxe5 Bxe5 14 Bh6, after which White has good compensation with the black king stuck in the centre of the board. He has a simple plan of Qf3 and Rae1, when Black's king will be extremely exposed.

11 c3

11 c4 is also possible, trying to bind the centre; e.g. 11...Nb6 (or 11...Nc7 12 Be3 0-0 13 Qb3) 12 Be3! with a slight advantage. The pawn on c4 is immune due to the check on a4.

11...Bg4

11...0-0 is a better try according to Bangiev, but White retains a slight edge after 12 Qb3 with his central control and more active pieces, while the bishop on g7 is blocked out of the game.

12 Qb3! (Diagram 17)

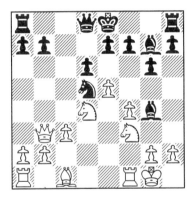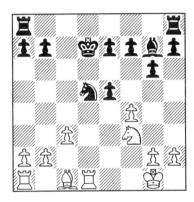

Diagram 17 (B)	Diagram 18 (B)
Aiming at b7 and f7	Keeping up the pressure

From here the queen hits the b7-pawn, which Black's previous move left undefended, and also generates x-rays down to the f7-square.

12...Bxf3 13 Nxf3 dxe5

Swapping queens with 13...Qb6+ 14 Qxb6 Nxb6 does not relieve Black's suffering after 15 exd6 exd6 16 f5!. However, if White now recaptures the pawn on e5 then 14...Qb6+ leaves Black close to having equalized.

14 Qb5+!?

41

14 Kh1!? is an interesting try if White wants to retain the queens. The threat is Rd1 (which was pointless before because of the reply ...Qb6+) and it is difficult to find a good move for Black: 14...exf4? loses to 15 Rd1 e6 16 c4, while after 14...Nb6 either 15 Nxe5 or 15 fxe5 provides White with a nice initiative.

14...Qd7 15 Qxd7+ Kxd7 16 Rd1! (Diagram 18)

Maintaining the pressure despite the trade of queens.

16...e4

If 16...Kc6 17 fxe5 Rad8 (or 17...Rhd8) 18 Ng5 highlights the weakness of the f7-square and White holds the advantage.

17 Ng5

White does not take the knight on d5 as he would have to give back the piece on f3.

17...Kc6 18 Nxf7 Rhf8 19 Ng5

The strong Polish GM re-establishes material parity with a much better structure, so Black is forced to try to exchange some of the pawns.

19...Nxf4 20 Bxf4 Rxf4 21 Re1

21 Ne6 would win after 21...Rf7? 22 Rd8!, but Black has the clever 21...Rf6!, which saves the piece by trapping the knight on g7: 22 Nxg7 Rg8 23 Rd4 Rxg7 24 Rxe4 Rgf7 and Black is okay, as his play down the f-file and more active king make up for his inferior pawn structure.

21...Rf5 22 Nxe4 Rd8 (Diagram 19)

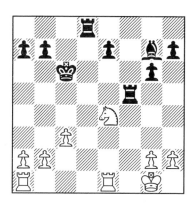

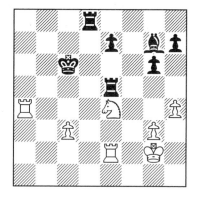

Diagram 19 (W)

Black has almost equalized

Diagram 20 (B)

White plays on and on

Black has almost equalized, but White can continue playing against the weak e7-pawn.

23 Re2 b5 24 g3 a5 25 a4!?

Bringing the a1-rook into play against Black's queenside.

25...bxa4 26 Rxa4 Rd1+ 27 Kg2 Kb5 28 b3 Rb1 29 Rea2 Rxb3 30 Rxa5+ Kc6 31 Ra8

White has traded his positional advantage for threats down the a-file and Black has to worry about the safety of his king.

31...Re5 32 Kf3 Rb1 33 Re2 Rf1+ 34 Kg2 Rf8 35 Ra6+ Kc7 36 Ra7+ Kc6 37 h4 Rd8 38 Kf3 Rf8+ 39 Kg2 Rd8 40 Ra4 (Diagram 20)

Perhaps White should not win this position, objectively speaking, but he can still torture Black with his strong central knight and passed c-pawn.

 TIP: In endings the outside passed pawn (that is the pawn furthest from the remaining pawns) is a strong asset, as it can be used to divert the opponent's king in order to hoover up the remaining pawns.

40...Kb5 41 Rea2 Kc6?! 42 Ng5!

Taking advantage of Black's misplaced pieces. Black cannot both defend the h7-pawn and prevent the knight moving into f7 to fork the rooks.

42...Re3 43 Nxh7 Rdd3 44 Rg4 Be5 45 Ra6+ Kc7 46 Raxg6

White has converted his initiative into two connected passed pawns and now finishes the game swiftly.

46...Rxc3 47 R4g5 Rc2+ 48 Kh3 Bf4 49 Rg4 Bd6 50 Ng5 Ree2 51 Ra4 Rh2+ 52 Kg4 Rhg2 53 Ne4 Be5 54 Ra7+ 1-0

Game 8
☐ **G.Jones** ■ **M.Agopov**
European Team Championship, Crete 2007

---

1 e4 c5 2 Nc3 Nc6 3 f4 g6 4 Nf3 Bg7 5 Bb5 Nd4 6 0-0 Nxb5 7 Nxb5 d6 8 d3 (Diagram 21)

In the previous game White opted for an immediate d2-d4, but I decided to keep to a true Grand Prix spirit with 8 d3, keeping the centre closed before attacking on the kingside.

8...Nf6

In the absence of a2-a4 Black can take the opportunity to advance on the queenside; for example, 8...a6 9 Nc3 b5 10 Qe1 b4 11 Nd1 a5, but then 12 Ne3 Bb7 13 Rb1 Nf6 14 c4 bxc3 15 bxc3 Rb8 16 c4 curtailed Black's queenside ambitions, and 16...0-0 17 Bd2 a4 18 Bc3 Bc6 19 Rxb8 Qxb8 20 f5 Nd7 21 Bxg7 Kxg7 22 Qg3 left White with a strong attack in M.Hebden-Gil.Hernandez, Havana 1993.

9 Qe1

Preparing to swing the queen over to the kingside.

9 e5!? is also interesting, trying to put pressure on Black's position straight away. Play continues 9...dxe5 10 fxe5 Nd5 (10...Ng4 11 Bf4 a6 12 Nc3 Nxe5 13 Nxe5 Qd4+ 14 Kh1 Bxe5 15 Bxe5 Qxe5 16 Qf3 0-0 17 Rae1 Qd6 18 Qe3 b6 19 Qxe7 Qxe7 20 Rxe7 was slightly better for White in E.Pinter-Z.Efimenko, Balatonlelle 2000) 11 Qe1! **(Diagram 22)** and then:

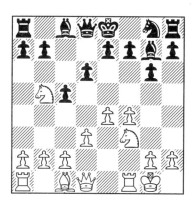

Diagram 21 (B)	Diagram 22 (B)
A standard Grand Prix set-up	Another way for White

a) 11...h6 12 Qf2 Qb6?! (12...b6 looks more sensible) 13 c4! Nb4 14 Ne1 Be6 15 Be3 Na6 16 b4! saw Black in trouble in M.Al Modiahki-Vl.Georgiev, Andorra 1999.

b) 11...Qd7!? 12 Nc3 Nb4 13 Qf2 b6 and now 14 a3 (the adventurous 14 Ng5 0-0 15 Nxf7?, with ideas of 16 Nh6+ Bxh6 17 Bxh6 and threats down the f-file, fails to 15...Qe8! 16 Nh6+ Bxh6 17 Bxh6 Rxf2 18 Rxf2 Bf5 and wins) 14...Nc6 15 Bf4 0-0 16 Rae1 is slightly better for White.

c) 11...0-0 might be a slight mistake as it falls in with White's plans: 12 Qh4 f6 (Black understandably wants to stop White's attack gathering even more momentum but this has a tactical drawback; instead 12...Qd7 13 Nc3 Nb4 was seen in J.Plaskett-Wl.Schmidt, Trnava 1984, when 14 Rf2 leaves White with a comfortable advantage: his plan is Ne4 and Bh6 to continue his attack) 13 exf6 exf6 14 Qc4 a6 (Degraeve has had success in this line before: 14...b6?! 15 Nc7! Qxc7 16 Qxd5+ Kh8 17 Qxa8 Bb7 18 Qxa7 Ra8 19 Bf4 Qc6 20 Qxa8+ Bxa8 21 Rae1 and White was clearly better in J.M.Degraeve-M.Velcheva, Metz 2000) 15 Nc7 Qxc7 16 Qxd5+ Kh8 17 Be3 b6 (giving up two rooks for the queen as otherwise Black would just go a pawn down) 18 Qxa8 Bb7 19 Qxf8+ Bxf8, and White's two rooks are better than the queen in this position with the open e-file and semi-open f-file. J.M.Degraeve-E.Djingarova, Metz 2001, continued 20 Bd2! (targeting the weak f6-pawn) 20...b5 21 Rae1 Qc6 22 Re2 b4?! 23 Ne5 Qd5? (but if 23...fxe5 24 Rxf8+ Kg7 25 Ref2 Qe6 26

Be3 with a clear advantage) 24 Rxf6 Kg8 25 Ng4 Qd4+ 26 Ref2 Bg7 27 Nh6+ Kh8 28.Rd6 and Black resigned.

9...0-0 10 f5! (Diagram 23)

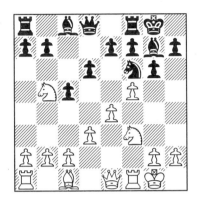

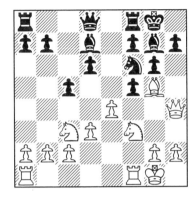

Diagram 23 (B)	Diagram 24 (B)
The familiar pawn break	White threatens 14 Nd5

10 Kh1 was seen in S.Iuldachev-S.Poobesh Anand, Commonwealth Championship, Mumbai 2003, which continued 10...Bd7 11 Nc3 Bc6 12 f5 b5 13 Qh4 b4 14 Ne2 e6 15 Bg5 with a typically good game for White. Nevertheless, Kh1 does not seem necessary yet, and instead White can continue his attack.

10...Bd7

In the post-mortem we spent a long time around here trying to come up with some improvements for Black, as the way the game goes he is left with an extremely passive and depressing position to play.

WARNING: As we have seen before 10...gxf5 is always a very risky pawn to take; for instance, 11 Qh4 Qb6 12 Nc3 c4+ 13 Kh1 cxd3 14 cxd3 fxe4 15 Ng5 h6 16 Ngxe4 leaves the black king exposed.

Another problem is that after 10...e6 White can make use of the knight on b5 by attacking the d6-pawn: 11 Bf4 e5 12 Bg5 Qb6 13 c4 a6 14 Nc3 Qxb2 15 Rb1 Qa3 16 Rb3 Qa5 17 Qh4 and for the rather useless b2-pawn White has a decisive attack.

Possibly 10...a6 is more accurate, as this would remove the threat to d6 after a later ...e7-e6, but it does not help Black develop his queenside pieces.

11 Nc3 e6

11...b5 12 Qh4 Re8 13 Bh6 Bh8 14 Ng5 gave White a strong attack in F.Sirch-T.Mackensy, German League 2002.

12 Qh4 exf5

45

If Black does not take this pawn then White's attack continues unhindered, but now a forced line ensues which gives White a nice advantage.

13 Bg5 (Diagram 24) 13...h6

Not 13...Be6 14 exf5 Bxf5? 15 Nd5 and wins, while 14...gxf5 seems too ugly for Black to contemplate. He is still no nearer to getting out of the deadly h4-d8 pin and will probably have to sacrifice his h-pawn so as not to drop a piece.

14 Bxh6 Nh7

Black has other options here, but I believe White has the better game after all of them.

My idea after 14...Ng4 was to play 15 Bg5 (15 Bxg7 isn't so clear after 15...Qxh4 16 Nxh4 Kxg7 17 exf5 Ne3!) 15...f6 (15...Bf6? 16 Nd5 is winning) 16 Bd2 with a slight advantage. The attempt to force things with 16 exf5 fxg5 17 Nxg5?, hoping for 17...Rxf5? 18 Qh7+ Kf8 19 Qxg6 Bd4+ 20 Kh1 Nf2+ 21 Rxf2! Bxf2 (or 21...Rxf2 22 Nh7+ Ke7 23 Nd5 mate) 22 Nh7+ Ke7 23 Nd5+! Rxd5 24 Qf6+ Ke8 25 Qf8 mate, fails to 17...Bh6!. Instead 17 Qxg4 Bxf5 18 Qxg5 would win a pawn, but here Black has two strong bishops in compensation.

Fritz's suggestion of 14...Bxh6 gets Black into a lot of trouble after 15 Qxh6 c4 (or if 15...Ng4 16 Qf4, when White has the superior structure, more space, a safer king and better squares for his pieces, in particular his knights) 16 Ng5 Qb6+ 17 Kh1 Bc6 18 Rf3! and Black is powerless against the old fashioned rook swing; e.g. 18...Qxb2 19 Rb1 Qxc3 20 Rh3 and mates.

15 Bxg7 Kxg7

If 15...Qxh4 16 Nxh4 Kxg7 17 exf5 wins a pawn.

16 Qg3

Increasing the pressure, both against Black's king and his backward d6-pawn, whereas swapping queens would let Black survive.

16...Qb6 17 b3

I wanted to keep everything safe and retain my advantage but 17 Nd5! might be more accurate. Then 17...Qxb2 18 Qxd6 fxe4 19 Rab1 Qxc2 20 Ne5, as suggested by Richard Palliser, would have given me a strong initiative.

17...c4+ 18 Kh1 cxd3 19 cxd3 Rae8 (Diagram 25)

Black has developed all his pieces and has almost equalized, but White still holds the advantage with a safer king and superior pawn structure, while his two minor pieces are more useful than Black's.

Instead 19...Nf6!? 20 exf5 Bxf5 21 Nh4 Be6 doesn't appear to allow a kingside knockout, but 22 Nf5+ Bxf5 23 Rxf5 Qd4! 24 Raf1 Qxc3 25 Rxf6 Qxf6 26 Rxf6 Kxf6 27 Qxd6+ Kg7 gives White the advantage in the ending with queen and pawn vs. the two rooks.

20 Nh4 fxe4 21 dxe4 Re5 22 Nf3 Re6 23 Rad1

Targeting the weak d-pawn.

23...Qc5 24 Rd3 Nf6 25 Ng5 Re5 26 Qf3

Perhaps 26 Rxf6!? Rxg5 (26...Kxf6 27 Nh7+ Kg7 28 Nxf8 Kxf8) 27 Qxd6 was a better way to retain the advantage.

26...Ng4 27 Rd5 Rxd5?

Played more or less instantly, but here 27...Qe3! would have equalized for Black, as after 28 Rxd6 Rxg5 29 Rxd7 Qxf3 30 gxf3 Black has 30...Nxh2! (and if 31 Rf2?? Nxf3! forces mate).

28 Nxd5 f5

Too weakening, but even after 28...f6 White keeps a clear advantage with 29 Qf4! (threatening h2-h3; the immediate 29 h3 Ne5 30 Qf4 can be met by 30...Nd3, though White is still better after 31 Qd2) 29...Qc8 30 Nf3 Ne5 31 Nd4.

29 h3 Ne5 30 Qf4

Threatening to penetrate on the h-file.

30...Nd3?

30...Rh8 may be forced, but White still has much the better chances after 31 Rd1.

31 Qh4 Rh8 32 Ne6+! (Diagram 26) 32...Bxe6 33 Qf6+ Kh7 34 Qe7+

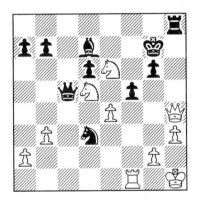

Diagram 25 (W)	Diagram 26 (B)
White holds the advantage	Clearing the way for the queen

My original idea was 34 Ne7, but just before I played it I noticed Black had the interesting 34...Nf4!, which is indirectly defended by the check on c1. White should still be winning after 35 Qg5 but this position would require more work.

34...Kh6 35 Qxe6

Black's king is far too weak and cannot survive long.

35...f4

If 35...Nf2+ 36 Kh2 fxe4 37 Nf4 Qf5 38 Qxf5 gxf5 39 Rxf2 wins, while *Fritz's* suggestion of 35...Qc8 does not help Black's cause after 36 exf5 Qxe6 37 fxe6 Re8 38 Rf6 as the passed pawn is simply too strong.

36 Qf6 Qc8

This loses instantly, but Black had no way of preventing Ne7 or Nxf4 anyway.

37 Ne7 Qe8 38 Nf5+ 1-0

Game 9
☐ **G.Jones** ■ **T.Gelashvili**
European Team Championship, Crete 2007

---

1 e4 c5 2 Nc3 Nc6 3 f4 g6 4 Nf3 Bg7 5 Bb5 Nd4 6 0-0 e6

A logical move by Black who simply wishes to develop his kingside. If White allows this then Black will have comfortable equality.

7 e5! (Diagram 27)

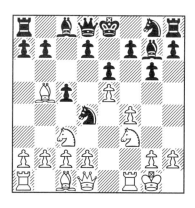
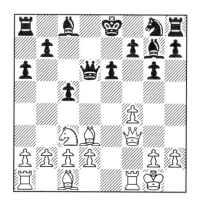

Diagram 27 (B)	**Diagram 28 (W)**
Pinpointing the weak d6-square	Black's best defence

Exploiting the weakness on d6 which Black's previous move created.

7...a6

Otherwise White will take on d4 and play Ne4, jumping into d6.

8 Bd3 d5?!

Instead:

a) 8...d6!? is a rare move, but the following line given by Richard Palliser seems good for White: 9 Ne4! Nf5 (or 9...dxe5 10 fxe5 Nxf3+ 11 Qxf3 and e5 is inedible due to Qxf7 mate) 10 g4!? d5 11 Nxc5 Qb6 12 b4! Qxb4 13 Nb3!? Nfe7 14 Nbd4. Black still has to develop his kingside, while his queen is misplaced on b4 allowing White to gain further tempi as it retreats. White's kingside expansion should also help in his attack.

b) 8...Nxf3+ 9 Qxf3 d5 10 exd6 Qxd6 **(Diagram 28)** is Black's best: 11 b3 Nf6 12 Bb2 0-0 13 Na4 Nd5 14 Bxg7 Kxg7 15 Be4 (another option is 15 Qf2 b6 16 Be4 Rb8 17 d4! with a slight advantage) 15...Nf6! (15...b5?! dropped a pawn to 16 Bxd5! exd5 17 Qc3+ d4 18 Qxc5 in S.Kindermann-L.Vogt, Austrian League 1999) and now 16 Bxb7 was too ambitious in G.Jones-K.Stokke, Pula 2007, while 16 Qc3 Qd4+ 17 Qxd4 cxd4 18 Nb6 Rb8 is just equal. So White should seek an improvement, either on the previous move (such as 15 Qf2), or here 16 Rf2, cutting out the annoying checks on the a7-g1 diagonal and defending d2, though I'm not sure it's enough for an advantage after 16...Rb8 17 Re1 b5 18 Nb2 Rd8 19 Nd3 c4.

9 Nxd4 cxd4 10 Ne2 (Diagram 29)

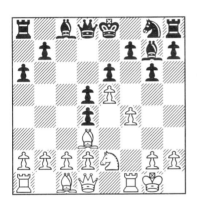

Diagram 29 (B)
The d4-pawn is vulnerable

Diagram 30 (B)
White plans Qf2 and Qh4

Now Black has a very vulnerable pawn on d4 which cannot be defended indefinitely.

10...Qb6

Black has to try ...f7-f6 over the next few moves, but each time White can retain the advantage; e.g. 10...f6 11 exf6 (11 c3, sacrificing the e-pawn, might also be investigated) 11...Bxf6 12 b4 Ne7 13 Bb2 Qb6 14 a3 Bd7 15 Qe1 Bb5 16 Bxb5+ axb5 17 Qf2 Nc6 18 c3 0-0 19 cxd4 and White was clearly better in T.Wipperman-P.Ostermeyer, Pfullendorf 2003.

11 Qe1 Ne7 12 b3

Developing the bishop to b2, while the possibility of Ba3 is also useful in some positions.

12...Nc6

If 12...f6 13 Bb2!? (or just 13 exf6 Bxf6 14 a4 Nc6 15 Qg3) 13...fxe5 14 fxe5 Bxe5 (14...Nc6 15 Qf2 also looks promising for White) 15 Qf2 Nc6 16 Qf7+ Kd8 17 Nf4 gives White a strong attack.

13 Bb2 0-0?

13...f6 was essential, when 14 Kh1 (14 exf6 Bxf6 15 f5 gxf5 16 Nf4 is rather unclear) 14...fxe5 (if 14...0-0? 15 Nxd4! Nxd4 16 Qe3 regains the piece and leaves White a pawn up with a pleasant position) 15 fxe5 **(Diagram 30)** was my idea and now:

a) 15...Nxe5 16 Qf2 Rf8 (or 16...Qc7 17 Nxd4 Bd7 18 Qh4) 17 Qh4 is clearly good for White with the black king stuck in the centre. There's no need to enter the complications of 16 Bxd4 Nxd3 17 Qh4!? (17 Bxb6 Nxe1 18 Raxe1 is just equal) 17...Bxd4 (after 17...Qc7 18 Bxg7 Qxg7 19 cxd3 Black has problems with his king, bad bishop and weak e6-pawn) 18 Nxd4 g5 (18...Ne5? 19 Qf6 Qxd4 20 Qxh8+ Kd7 21 c3 or 18...Nc5? 19 Qf6 Rg8 20 Qf7+ wins) 19 Qh5+ Kd7 20 Qf7+ Kd6 21 Qg7 which is extremely messy, though I feel White still should be doing well here as Black is way behind on development and his king is floating around in the middle of the board.

b) 15...Bxe5 16 Qf2 Qc7 (16...Bd7 17 Qf7+ Kd8 18 Nf4 again leaves White with a very promising position) 17 Nxd4 Qg7 18 Nxe6! (I have to admit this is the computer's suggestion, but it seems very strong) 18...Bxe6 19 Bxe5 Nxe5 20 Qd4! and Black has no defence to Re1, regaining the piece and leaving White a pawn up.

14 Nxd4! Nb4

If 14...Nxd4 15 Qe3 Ne2+ 16 Bxe2 Qxe3+ 17 dxe3 and White is clearly better, a pawn up in the queenless middlegame.

15 Qe3 Nxd3 16 Qxd3 Bd7 17 Qe3 (Diagram 31)

White is again a pawn up and his knight on d4 completely controls the position. Maybe Black has to try opening the f-file with 17...f6 when at least his bishop on g7 can contribute something to the game, but his position is still terrible.

17...a5 18 Ba3

Reactivating the bishop. My plan was to control certain important squares on this diagonal and then at the opportune moment trade dark-squared bishops, when my kingside attack would be stronger.

18...Rfc8 19 Be7 a4 20 b4 a3 21 c3 Rc4 22 Rf3

With the queenside locked, White can turn his hand to the kingside and, indeed, Gelashvili doesn't last long there. Perhaps with hindsight I could have spent a tempo on 22 Rb1, cutting out any tricks on the queenside before launching my kingside attack. Black has no useful way to improve his position and must wait anyway.

22...Bf8 23 Bf6?

This is a mistake, allowing Black back in the game. I overlooked a saving resource which my opponent also missed later in the game. Instead, I should trade bishops and gone into an ending with 23 Bxf8 Rxf8 24 f5! exf5 25 Nxf5 Qxe3+ 26 Nxe3 Rcc8 27 Nxd5 when White's extra two pawns should be winning fairly easily. However, I wanted to mate him!

23...Bxb4! 24 Rh3 (Diagram 32)

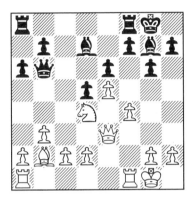

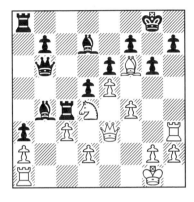

Diagram 31 (B)	**Diagram 32 (B)**
The d4-pawn has fallen	White threatens 25 Rxh7

24 Rb1 Bxc3! 25 Rxb6 Bxd4 is Black's cunning trick, after which White has only a slight advantage.

24...h5?

24...Bf8! 25 Rxh7 Kxh7 26 Qh3+ Bh6 27 Bg5 Rh8! is the move both of us missed, when Black has survived and is even winning. Instead, 25 Qd3! is Richard Palliser's suggestion to continue my attack and leads to some interesting variations, the main line being 25...Ra5 26 g4! h6 27 Kg2 Qb2 28 Rb1 Qxa2 29 Rxb7; e.g. 29...Rxd4 30 cxd4 Bb5 31 Qc3 Qb1 32 Rf3 a2 33 Qc7 Be8 34 Rxb1 axb1Q 35 Qxa5 and White should convert his material advantage.

25 f5!

Now it's all over. After a blip by me and then my opponent, the position is winning again, as White's attack is simply too strong.

25...Rxd4

25...Kh7 26 Rxh5+! gxh5 27 Qg5 is mate in a few moves, or if 25...Bf8 26 Rxh5! gxh5 27 Qg5+ Kh7 28 Qxh5+ Bh6 29 Qxf7+ etc.

26 Qh6! 1-0

Black has no useful discovered checks and cannot prevent mate on either g7 or h8.

Game 10
☐ **M.Adams** ■ **V.Anand**
FIDE World Championship, Groningen 1997

1 e4 c5 2 Nc3 Nc6 3 f4 g6 4 Nf3 Bg7 5 Bb5 Nd4 6 0-0 a6 (Diagram 33)

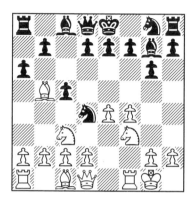
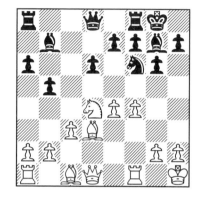

Diagram 33 (W)	Diagram 34 (W)
Black plays 6...a6	White should target the queenside

The main alternative to 6...Nxb5.

7 Bd3 d6

7...b5 is examined in the next game.

8 Nxd4 cxd4

8...Bxd4+ is inaccurate as the bishop finds itself misplaced on d4 and White can exploit it to reorganize. For example, 9 Kh1 e6 (if 9...Nf6?! 10 Ne2 or 9...Nh6 10 Ne2 Bg7 11 Qe1, while after 9...Bg7 10 Qf3 Nf6 11 e5 Ng4 12 Bc4 dxe5? 13 Bxf7+! Kxf7 14 fxe5+ White recouped his piece with a clear advantage in S.Iuldachev-K.A.Grigorian, Ashkhabad 1996) 10 Ne2 Bg7 11 c3 Ne7 12 Bc2 0-0 13 d4 cxd4 14 cxd4 and White is somewhat better, T.L.Petrosian-T.Balkhamishvili, Batumi 2001.

9 Ne2 Nf6 10 Kh1

Simply sidestepping with the king so that White may be able to capture on d4 at some point.

10 c3!? has also been tried. White wishes to develop his queenside and this seems like a logical choice: 10...dxc3 11 dxc3 (11 bxc3 can be compared to Hodgson-Petursson in the notes to Game 12 and seems natural as we are told to capture towards the centre – in this case, however, Black will get good play against the weak c3-pawn after White moves his d-pawn, e.g. 11...0-0 12 Bc2 Qc7 13 Qe1 b5 14 Bb2

Bb7 15 d3 Ng4) 11...0-0 and now:

a) 12 a4?! holds back Black's ...b7-b5 for a while, but cannot be recommended as once Black achieves the break he will be able to play down the open a-file: 12...b6! 13 c4 Bb7 14 Nc3 b5! 15 axb5 axb5 16 Rxa8 Qxa8 17 Nxb5 Bxe4 leaves Black with the advantage.

 TIP: When attacking on the opposite side to your opponent, do not allow your opponent more open files to attack down than necessary.

b) 12 Kh1!? b5 13 Nd4! (centralizing the knight and provoking Black to play ...e7-e5 which would block in his g7-bishop; i.e. 13...e5?! 14 fxe5 dxe5 15 Nf3 with a slight advantage, and White can also consider 14 Nc6!?) 13...Bb7 **(Diagram 34)**. White should probably play on the queenside in this particular position and go for a2-a4 to target the a6 and b5-pawns. He can think about playing e4-e5 at some point but has to be very careful, as opening the centre will allow Black's bishops to become extremely powerful. For instance, 14 e5?! cannot be recommended as it allows Black's b7-bishop to come to life, directed towards White's king; i.e. 14...dxe5 15 fxe5 Qd5! and Black holds the trumps of the position.

14 Qe2 is better, simply defending the pawn on e4, after which 14...Nd7 15 Nb3! (countering ...Nc5 and preparing a2-a4) 15...e5!? 16 f5! d5 17 Be3! dxe4! 18 Bc2 Bd5! 19 Rfd1 Bxb3? (19...Nf6 was necessary and unclear) 20 axb3 gxf5 21 Qh5 was good for White in J.M.Degraeve-I.Nataf, French League 2001.

Instead, 14...e6! was suggested by GMs Bacrot and Pavlovic, again planning to reroute the knight round to c5, supported by ...Qc7. Then 15 a4 bxa4! 16 Rxa4 a5! 17 Rd1 Nd7 18 Bc2 Nc5 19 Ra3 Qb6 20 Nb3 Nxb3 21 Rxb3 Qc7 is equal according to Nataf, though 17 Nb5!? might be a better try for an advantage.

10...Nd7

Black defends d4 and threatens the annoying ...Nc5. 10...0-0 allows White an easy plan in 11 Nxd4!? Nxe4 12 Bxe4 Bxd4 13 Qf3 (not yet 13 c3?! d5!?) 13...Rb8 14 c3 Bg7 15 f5 b5 16 d4 with a nice position in Art.Minasian-K.Arakhamia, World Team Championship, Lucerne 1997.

11 b4!? (Diagram 35)

A multipurpose move. With his d-pawn blocked White cannot develop the c1-bishop on the c1-h6 diagonal and so plans to move it to b2, attacking the weak d4-pawn. It also stops Black playing his knight to c5 where it would terrorize the d3-bishop.

11 Bc4 is another try but it has not been successful for White: 11...d5!? reaches a position similar to Polgar-Topalov (Game 12) and Black has equalized.

11...0-0 12 Bb2 Qb6 13 Rb1!

Indirectly defending the b4-pawn, since 13...Qxb4?! 14 Bxd4 Qa3 15 Bxg7 Kxg7 16 Nc3 would leave White with a lead in development, the centre, an active rook on b1 and a promising attack on the kingside, while Black no longer has his dark-squared bishop which is a key defender in such positions.

13...Nb8!?

Rerouting the knight to c6 and allowing the c8-bishop to develop.

14 c3

14 f5 might be an improvement as it allows the white knight to use the f4-square and then to hop to d5. It also keeps the c8-bishop out of g4, where it could be exchanged for White's good knight.

14...Nc6

Keeping the d4-pawn on the board. 14...dxc3?! 15 Nxc3 would allow White's knight to d5 and then, after the trade of dark-squared bishops, the black king will start to feel draughty.

15 h3

White does not want Black to be able to play ...Bg4, trading off his worse bishop and relieving the tension on the d4-pawn – though in this case 14 h3 Nc6 15 c3 might have been a more accurate move order.

> **TIP: When you have the initiative and more space you should try to keep as many pieces on the board as possible, as your opponent's will be short of squares in a cramped position.**

Here 15 a4 Bg4 is just equal, while 15 cxd4!? Nxd4 (if 15...Bg4 16 d5 Bxb2 17 Rxb2 Nd4 18 Qe1 keeps the extra pawn) 16 f5!? Nxe2 17 Qxe2 Bxb2 18 Rxb2 Qd4 19 Rb3 or 19 Rc2!? is unclear.

15...Be6 16 a4 Rac8 (Diagram 36)

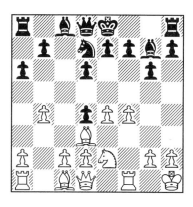

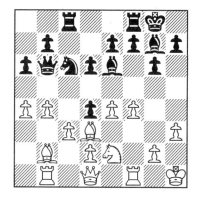

Diagram 35 (B)	Diagram 36 (W)
A multipurpose move	The game is roughly equal

Black has completed his development and holds rough equality.

17 Qe1!

Threatening Qf2, pinning the d-pawn to the black queen, so Black is forced to trade on c3.

17...dxc3 18 Bxc3 Bxc3 19 dxc3

19 Nxc3 is not so successful now as Black can make use of the d4-square, while the bishop on e6 stops the white knight from utilizing d5.

19...f6!

A good move by Anand. White was threatening to push his f-pawn to f5, hitting the bishop and driving it from the a2-g8 diagonal, which would allow the white knight to use the d5-square once more. White could play a further f5-f6 at some point, exploiting the fact that the black kingside is now weak without the g7-bishop.

Instead, Bangiev notes 19...f5?! 20 exf5 Bxf5 21 Bxf5 Rxf5 22 Ng3 Rf7 23 Qe6 with a good attack, while 19...Qc7 20 Qh4 Nd8 21 f5 Bc4 22 Bxc4 Qxc4 23 Nf4! gives White a clear advantage.

20 a5 Qc7 21 Qg3

The one downside of 19...f6 was that it weakened the g6-pawn, so Adams starts to target it.

21...Bf7

If 21...Rcd8 22 f5 Bf7 23 fxg6 hxg6 24 Nf4 Ne5 25 c4 and White is slightly better according to Bangiev.

22 h4!?

22 f5 would give Black's knight an extremely strong outpost on e5, so White prefers to advance the h-pawn against the black king position.

22...Kh8 23 Qh3! (Diagram 37)

Another useful multipurpose move. White has several ideas here: to continue the kingside attack with h4-h5 followed by Ng3, or play on the queenside with c4 and b5, forcing the knight to retreat, and then try manoeuvring his knight to e6 via d4.

23...Rcd8!

With the ideas of ...d6-d5 and perhaps ...Qc8, challenging the white queen on the h3-c8 diagonal.

24 c4

Preventing ...d6-d5, while 24...Qc8 25 Qxc8 Rxc8 leaves White with more space and a slight advantage in the queenless middlegame. So Black finds counterplay elsewhere:

24...b6! 25 axb6 Qxb6 26 b5 axb5 27 cxb5 Na5

If 27...Nd4?! 28 Qe3 is awkward for Black.

28 h5!?

White continues the attempt to crash through on the kingside.

28...gxh5 29 Ng3 Qe3

Defending the h5-pawn as 30 Nxh5 would now lose a piece after 30...Qxh3+.

30 Rf3 Qc5 31 b6

With the idea of Rb5 when the rook will swing across to the kingside. 31 Nf5!? was also worth considering.

31...Nb3

Blocking the b-file, so White continues his attack on the other side.

32 e5! dxe5

32...Nd2? leaves h7 too exposed after 33 Nxh5!, and if Black takes either rook 34 Nxf6! wins immediately.

33 Nxh5 (Diagram 38)

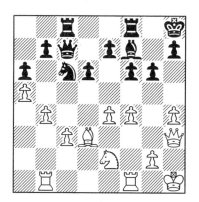

Diagram 37 (B)

White has various ideas here

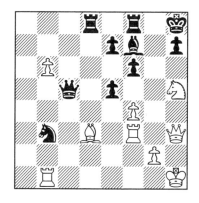

Diagram 38 (B)

A complicated position

The position is extremely complicated. Black is theoretically a pawn up but his king is very exposed and most players would crumble and lose straight away. Anand shows why he's been in the top three in the world for over a decade.

33...e4

The alternative was 33...Bxh5 and then:

a) 34 Qxh5? runs into 34...e4! winning for Black.

b) 34 Bxh7!? exf4! seems to hold; e.g. 35 Rfxb3 (not 35 Bf5? Kg7! and Black wins as the f4-pawn prevents Rg3+) 35...Kxh7 36 b7 f3!? 37 g4 (if 37 Rxf3 Kg7 38 Rf5 Qc2 or 37 gxf3 Qe5) 37...Qc2 38 b8Q (38 Qxh5+? Kg7) 38...Rxb8 39 Rxb8 Rxb8 40 Rxb8

Qd1+ 41 Kh2 Qd6+ 42 Qg3 Bxg4.

c) 34 Rxb3! is the best try, but 34...e4! 35 Rb5 Qc1+ 36 Rf1 Qc8 37 Qxc8 Rxc8 38 b7 Rb8 defends since 39 Bxe4? allows 39...Be2 forking the rooks.

34 Bxe4 Nd2 35 Nxf6! h5 36 Rc3

Perhaps short of time Adams takes a draw by repetition. Instead, 36 Nd7! would leave him with the advantage, as after 36...Rxd7 37 Qxd7 Nxe4 38 b7! the strong b-pawn more than compensates for Black's knight and bishop vs. rook.

36...Qa5

Black has no choice since 36...Nxe4 37 Nxe4! is no good for him.

37 Ra3

Even here White could try 37 Nxh5!?, when the natural-looking 37...Qxh5? is re-futed by 38 Rb5!, but 37...Bxh5 38 Re1 Nxe4 39 Rxe4 Qf5 40 Qxf5 Rxf5 41 b7 Bg4!, planning to answer 42 Rc8 with 42...Rh5+ 43 Kg1 Rxc8, should hold for Black; e.g. 42 Rc7 Rf7 43 Rexe7 Rxe7 44 Rxe7 Rb8, followed by ...Kg8-f8-e8, ...Bd7 and ...Kd8 to expel the white rook and win the b-pawn.

37...Qc5 38 Rc3 Qa5 39 Ra3 ½-½

Game 11

☐ **G.Jones** ◼ **L.Van Wely**

Staunton Memorial, London 2007

---

1 e4 c5 2 Nc3 Nc6 3 f4 g6 4 Nf3 Bg7 5 Bb5 Nd4 6 0-0 a6 7 Bd3 b5 (Diagram 39)

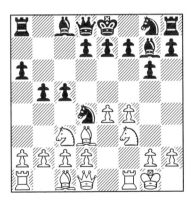
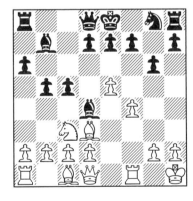

Diagram 39 (W)

Black tries to mix it up

Diagram 40 (B)

Fencing in the d4-bishop

A rare, but aggressive attempt by my high-rated opponent, trying to mix things up as quickly as possible.

8 Nxd4

Swapping off Black's best developed piece and forcing Black to make a decision.

8...Bxd4+

8...cxd4 again leaves Black with a weak pawn on d4, which can be ganged up on with Ne2, b2-b3 and Bb2; e.g. 9 Ne2 Bb7 10 b3 d6 11 a4 b4 12 Bb2 Nf6 13 Bxd4 0-0 14 a5! Nxe4 15 Bxg7 Kxg7 16 Ra4 Nc5 17 Qa1+ Kg8 18 Rxb4 and White is comfortably on top.

9 Kh1 Bb7 10 e5! (Diagram 40)

Trapping the bishop in on d4 and threatening both Ne2 and Be4.

10...Ra7?!

Black continues with his ultra-aggressive plan but he really needed to develop his kingside. In the post-mortem we looked at 10...Bxc3, but came to the conclusion that White still has the advantage: 11 dxc3 c4 (if 11...Nh6 either 12 a4 Qb6 13 Qe2 c4 14 Be4 or just 12 c4 is good for White) 12 Be2 Nh6 13 Bf3!, swapping off Black's strong light-squared bishop.

11 Be4

Black's last move prevented 11 Ne2? due to 11...Qa8 when White's king is in trouble.

11...Bxc3

11...Bxe4 12 Nxe4 would leave Black's bishop on d4 feeling rather vulnerable.

12 Bxb7 Bxb2?!

Again Loek plays far too ambitiously. However, 12...Rxb7 13 dxc3 is also very unpleasant for Black, as 13...Nh6? runs into 14 f5! Nxf5 15 g4! Nh4 16 Bg5 and the knight is trapped.

13 Bxb2 Rxb7

Black is a pawn up but his only piece not on its starting square is the rook on b7 – and that is actually worse placed since it is unprotected on b7, so White can gain a tempo for Qf3.

14 f5

Thematic: trying to open Black's kingside before he has time to develop his pieces.

14...Nh6 15 Qf3 (Diagram 41) 15...Qb6?

Black's final mistake and a fatal one. 15...Qc7 is forced, with the subtle idea that after 16 e6 f6 17 fxg6 hxg6 18 Bxf6 exf6 19 Qxf6 Qxh2+!! is playable swapping off queens after 20 Kxh2 Ng4+ 21 Kg3 Nxf6 22 Rxf6, though White still retains all the winning chances here. Otherwise White can try 17 exd7+ Qxd7 18 fxg6 hxg6 19 Rae1 or 16 f6 e6 17 d4 with good compensation for the pawn in either case.

16 e6!

Crashing through.

16...f6

16...Rg8 loses to 17 exf7+ Nxf7 18 fxg6, while after 16...0-0 I intended 17 Qh3 17...Nxf5 18 Rxf5 when White should be winning, though *Fritz* points out that 17 f6! is even stronger, e.g. 17...exf6 18 Qxf6 or 17...fxe6 18 fxe7! and wins.

17 fxg6 hxg6 18 Bxf6!

Another thematic move. Black's king is stripped of shelter completely and he won't even have a material advantage.

18...exf6

18...Rf8 19 Qg3 Rxf6 20 Rxf6 exf6 21 Qxg6+ is also hopeless for Black.

19 Qxf6 Rg8 20 Rae1! (Diagram 42)

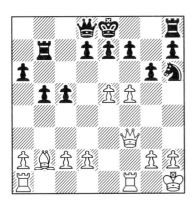

Diagram 41 (B)

The attack gains pace

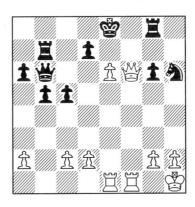

Diagram 42 (B)

All White's pieces join in

Using every piece in the attack. White threatens 21 Qf7+! against most moves; e.g. 20...Qd6 21 Qf7+ Kd8 (or 21...Nxf7 22 exf7+ Kf8 23 Re8+) 22 e7+ Kc7 23 Qxg8 Nxg8 24 e8N+! and wins. It's always nice to under-promote.

20...d5

Clearing the rank for the black rook so that if now 21 Qf7+? Rxf7 22 exf7+ Kd7 23 fxg8Q Nxg8 24 Rf7+ Kd6 defends.

21 Qg5!

Black has no way to retain his extra piece. If 21...Rh8 22 Qxg6+ Kd8 23 Qf6+ wins, while 21...Rh7 22 Rf7! Nxf7 23 exf7+ Kxf7 24 Qe7 is mate.

21...Re7 22 Qxh6

White now has an extra pawn (that mammoth one on e6!), a completely safe king and all his pieces on active squares, whereas Black's are uncoordinated and his king is exposed on e8.

22...Qa5

22...Rxe6 23 Qh7 Rf8 24 Qxg6+ is mate in six according to *Fritz*.

23 Rf6 Qxa2 24 Rxg6 Rf8 25 Qxf8+! 1-0

Black resigned since 25...Kxf8 26. Rf1+ Ke8 27 Rg8 is checkmate.

Game 12
☐ **J.Polgar** ■ **V.Topalov**
Dortmund 1996

1 e4 c5 2 Nc3 Nc6 3 f4 g6 4 Nf3 Bg7 5 Bb5 Nd4 6 Bd3!? (Diagram 43)

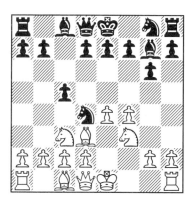 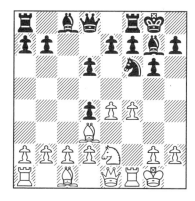

Diagram 43 (B)	Diagram 44 (B)
White plays 6 Bd3!?	Starting the standard attack

Rather than allow Black to take it, White retreats the bishop at once without waiting for ...a7-a6. It looks a little odd, blocking the d-pawn, but the bishop does at least defend the e-pawn and will not get hit by ...d5 (as it would on c4). White can see how Black develops before deciding which square the bishop will finally make its home on, and in the meantime can follow up (as in the 6 0-0 a6 7 Bd3 variation) with Nxd4, Ne2 and c2-c3 to develop the other bishop, or else b2-b3 and Bb2 at some point.

6...d6

6...e6?! allows White to exploit the hole newly created on d6: 7 Nxd4 cxd4 8 Nb5 d6 9 c3! dxc3 10 dxc3 (or 10 bxc3 intending Ba3 to target the weak d6-pawn) and now if 10...a6 (10...Ne7? 11 Nxd6+! Qxd6 12 Bb5+ picks up the black queen) 11 Qa4! gives Black some problems with his king.

7 Nxd4 cxd4 8 Ne2 Nf6

8...Nh6 is also interesting. Black keeps the long diagonal open so his bishop protects d4 and he will look to play ...d6-d5 and then use the f5-square for his knight. For example, 9 c3 dxc3 10 dxc3 0-0 11 0-0 d5 12 e5 Qb6+ 13 Kh1 Nf5 as in R.Dzindzichashvili-R.Hübner, Tilburg 1985, though after 14 Nd4!? Nxd4 15 Be3! Qxb2 16 Bxd4 White had good compensation for the pawn with his two centralized bishops and the black queen out of play.

9 0-0

9 Nxd4 Nxe4 10 Bxe4 Bxd4 11 c3 Bg7 12 d4 is equal according to Yermolinsky. But the immediate 9 c3!? dxc3 is a possibility, and then:

a) 10 dxc3 0-0 11 0-0 b5! 12 Ng3 (the pawn is poisoned: 12 Bxb5? Qb6+ 13 Nd4 e5 wins a piece) 12...a5 and Black equalized in D.Campora-M.Jukic, Bern 1989, which concluded 13 a3 Bd7 14 Qe2 Qb8 15 Bd2 Bc6 16 Rad1 Nd7 17 Rf2 ½-½.

b) 10 bxc3 seems more natural as we're taught to capture towards the centre, but here it's not obvious where White's bishops will go. J.Hodgson-M.Petursson, Reykjavik 1989, continued 10...0-0 11 0-0 b6! 12 Bc2 Bb7 13 d3 Qc7 14 Kh1 Rac8, and Black completed his development, while White's pieces still hadn't found ideal squares.

9...0-0 10 Qe1 (Diagram 44)

 NOTE: This natural-looking move was actually a novelty. Judit Polgar starts the typical kingside attack in the Grand Prix, though it seems harder to succeed with the bishop on d3 blocking in the one on c1.

Otherwise White can again try 10 c3!? (10 Nxd4? falls for the familiar trap 10...Qb6 11 c3 e5), though here Black can respond with 10...e5!? (10...dxc3 transposes to the previous note, while 10...Bg4 might lead to an unlikely repetition after 11 cxd4 Qb6 12 Kh1 Bxe2 13 Qxe2 Qxd4 14 Rb1 Qa4 15 a3 Qb3 16 Bc4 Qc2 17 Bd3 Qb3 etc), when 11 cxd4 exd4 leaves the e4-pawn vulnerable; for example, 12 b3 (or 12 b4 Re8 13 Ng3 h5 14 f5 h4 15 Ne2 g5 16 Bc2 d3 17 Bxd3 Nxe4 18 Bxe4 Bxa1 with a decisive advantage, C.Friis-J.Kristensen, Danish Junior Championships 1992) 12...Re8 13 Ng3 h5 14 f5 h4 15 Ne2 Nxe4 16 Bxe4 Rxe4 17 d3 Re5 18 fxg6 Bg4 19 exf7+ Kh7 and Black won in M.Basman-A.Adorjan, London 1975.

10...Nd7

Dropping the knight back to keep d4 protected and threaten 11...Nc5 hitting the bishop. 10...e5 11 b3 Re8 12 Bb2 is slightly better for White according to Bangiev.

11 Bc4

This move has been given both '!?' and '?' in annotations I have seen. (Polgar herself gave it '?'.) It makes sense to play Bc4 now, to complete development with d2-d3, as Black's knight retreat seems to rule out his responding with ...d6-d5, but Black plays it anyway!

Instead, 11 Qf2 Nc5! (Topalov's intention) 12 Nxd4 Nxd3 13 cxd3 Bd7 14 b3 Bb5 is a line from Judit's notes, where Black has at least enough compensation for the pawn with the two bishops, open lines and the superior pawn structure.

11...d5! (Diagram 45)

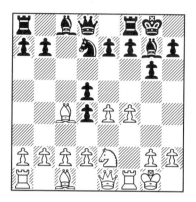 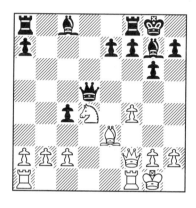

Diagram 45 (W)	Diagram 46 (B)
Black strikes back	Black has equalized

Topalov strikes out, attacking the bishop and forcing White to damage her centre. Bangiev suggests 11...Qc7 12 d3 Nb6 13 Bb3 Be6!?, targeting White's weak c2-pawn, as an alternative which results in very unclear positions; e.g. 14 c3 (if 14 Bxe6 fxe6 15 c4 dxc3 16 bxc3 Rac8 17 Bd2 e5 or 17...Na4 with counterplay) 14...dxc3 15 bxc3 (or 15 Nxc3 Bxb3 16 axb3 Qc5+ 17 Be3 Qb4 with the initiative) 15...Rac8 16 Bd2 Bd7 17 Qf2.

12 exd5

12 Bxd5 is the other way to capture the pawn, but then Black can win it back with 12...Nf6, since after the bishop moves the e4-pawn will be en prise: 13 Bb3 (or 13 Ng3 Nxd5 14 exd5 d3) 13...Nxe4 14 d3 Nd6 and Black is doing well as the e3-square is a major weakness for White.

12...Nb6 13 d3

Defending the bishop and starting to develop the queenside. 13 Bb3 is not so good, as 13...d3!? 14 cxd3 Nxd5 gives Black a strong initiative for the pawn, and he was also doing well after 13...a5 14 a4 Nxd5 15 d3 e6 16 Kh1 b6 17 Ng3 f5 in S.Weeramantry-A.Lein, US Open, Dearborn 1992.

13...Nxc4!

A brave attempt to play for the win! Instead, 13...Nxd5 14 Qf2 Nb6 15 Bb3 Qd6 is equal, but 14 Kh1! (Bangiev) offers White a slight advantage. The point is to re-route the knight from e2 to f3 via g1, from where it can jump to e5 or g5. For example, 14...Nb6 15 Bb3 Qd6 (or 15...a5 16 a4 Bd7 17 Bd2) 16 Ng1 Bd7 17 Nf3 Rac8 18 a4!, cutting out any ...Ba4 ideas, when White can play on both sides of the board and the plan Qh4, Ng5 and Ne4 looks promising.

14 dxc4 b5

Topalov continues in aggressive mode, attempting to open the h1-a8 diagonal for his c8-bishop, after which White must be careful about her king. Alternatively, 14...e6!? would win the pawn back, as after 15 dxe6 Bxe6 White cannot defend c4 with 16 b3 because of 16...d3! hitting the rook on a1 and the knight on e2, while 15 Qf2 exd5 16 Nxd4 dxc4 17 Be3 Re8 18 c3 is around equal and similar to the game. Black has the two bishops, but White has a good outpost on d4 which she can use for her knight or bishop.

15 Qf2!

White returns the pawn in order to complete her development, though she didn't really have a choice, as 15 cxb5 Qxd5 16 Ng3 Qxb5 (or 16...Bb7 17 Qe2 a6) 17 Qxe7 Re8 18 Qa3 Bb7 leaves all White's pieces misplaced and Black threatening a quick kingside onslaught.

15...bxc4 16 Nxd4 Qxd5 17 Be3 (Diagram 46)

Black has regained material parity and equalized. He has the two bishops and the semi-open b-file to play down if he wishes. White, on the other hand, has a good square for her knight on d4, which will be very hard to shift after she plays c2-c3, and can develop her rooks strongly on the central files.

17...a5

17...Bb7 allows White to play 18 f5, while 17...Rb8 doesn't achieve anything as White defends her b2-pawn with 18 c3 anyway. But 17...c3!? is interesting, sacrificing a pawn to weaken White's structure, when Black will have good compensation.

18 c3 Rd8

A tricky position has emerged. White needs to come up with a plan since the usual f4-f5 does not work here; i.e. 19 f5 Bxd4! 20 Bxd4 (not 20 fxg6? Bf6 and White has nothing for the piece) 20...Bxf5 and Black picks up the pawn.

After the natural 19 Rad1 Bf5! forces White into a tactical exchange: 20 Nxf5 Qxd1!? (20...Qxf5 is still equal) 21 Nxg7 (not 21 Rxd1? Rxd1+ 22 Qf1 Rxf1+ 23 Kxf1 gxf5 with an extra rook; but 21 Nxe7+ Kh8 22 Nc6 Rd6 23 Ne5 Qd5 24 Bd4 is possible, when White has some compensation for the exchange with a pawn and well placed bishop and knight) 21...Kxg7 (21...Qd5 22 Bd4 is clearly better for White as Black has no way to exploit the knight's odd placement on g7, e.g. 22...f6?! 23 Qe2! Kxg7 24 Qxe7+ Qf7 25 Bxf6+ Kg8 26 Qxf7+ Kxf7 27 Bxd8 and wins) 22 Bd4+ (forcing Black to return the exchange as his queen is now hanging) 22...Rxd4 23 Qxd4+ Qxd4+ 24 cxd4 Rb8 and White has to hold a slightly worse ending.

19 Qc2!?

Keeping an eye on the f5-square and defending the d1-square so that Rad1 can be played without the complications seen above.

19...e6

Topalov blocks in his own bishop but clamps down on the f5-square. Instead, 19...Bf5!? 20 Nxf5 Qxf5 21 Qxf5 gxf5 22 Rfd1 is somewhat better for White according to Bangiev, while 19...Bb7 again allows 20 f5.

20 Rad1 (Diagram 47)

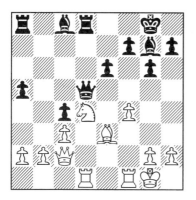

Diagram 47 (B)	Diagram 48 (B)
White centralizes her forces	Which way should the king go?

Centralizing the rook and threatening to move the knight, which would leave Black's queen skewered against the undefended rook on d8.

20...Qh5

Fritz's number one suggestion and an obvious move as Black shifts the queen from the line of fire. 20...Qh5 has been given a question mark in previous annotations, as now Polgar skilfully uses the squares on the queenside, which ...Qh5 left undefended, in order to activate her pieces. However, the alternative 20...Bb7 allows White to play 21 f5! after all, as the following analysis from Bangiev shows: 21...gxf5 (if 21...exf5 22 Nxf5 Qe6 23 Nh6+ Bxh6 24 Bxh6 and White has regained the initiative) 22 Nxf5 Qe4 (or 22...Qxg2+!? 23 Qxg2 Bxg2 24 Rxd8+ Rxd8 25 Kxg2 exf5 26 Rxf5) 23 Qxe4 Bxe4 24 Nxg7 Kxg7 25 Bd4+ with a slight advantage.

> **TIP: It is often not understood that opposite-coloured bishops, rather than making the game more drawish, give the side with the attack a clear advantage when other pieces are left on the board. This is because, to take this position as an example, Black cannot defend the dark squares around his king.**

21 Nc6!

Taking control of the d-file.

21...Rxd1

If 21...Re8 the knight takes up a strong post with 22 Ne5, as taking it would leave Black very weak on the dark squares.

22 Rxd1 Bb7

If 22...Bf6 then 23 Bd4.

23 Ne7+ (Diagram 48)

Allowing her rook to the seventh rank when Topalov's king begins to look in some difficulty.

23...Kh8?

The alternative 23...Kf8! seems to be just asking for trouble with Be3-c5; for example, 24 Rd7 Qb5 25 Qd2 (threatening Rd8+, as well as a2-a4 to overload the black queen) 25...Bd5 (as in the game) 26 Rc7 Rd8 27 Bc5 leaves White with a huge attack. But in fact the black king can take care of himself: 25...Ke8! 26 Rc7 Rd8 27 Qe2 Rd3 28 Nc8 Kd8! 29 Rxf7 Qd5 and suddenly Black is in charge. So White has to play 25 Rc7, but then 25...Bf6 26 Bc5 (26 a4 Qa6) 26...Kg7 27 Qd2 Re8 reorganizes the defence successfully.

24 Rd7! Qb5 25 Qd2

Now Rd8+ is a serious threat, so Topalov closes the d-file.

25...Bd5 26 Rc7

Threatening to take on d5 and then f7.

26...Be4?!

26...Rd8! is a better try, but White has various moves here retaining a big advantage; for instance:

a) 27 Nxd5 Qxd5 (if 27...Rxd5 28 Rc8+ Bf8 29 Qe2 Kg8 30 Rxc4) 28 Rxc4 (if 28 Qxd5 exd5 29 Rxf7 Rb8 30 Rd7 Kg8 31 Bc1 Bxc3! – Polgar) 28...Qxd2 29 Bxd2 Rxd2 (or 29...Bf6 30 Be3) 30 Rc8+ Bf8 31 Rxf8+ Kg7 32 Rb8 and White is a pawn up in the endgame, though Black might be able to grovel a draw.

d) 27 Bd4!? f6 28 Qe1 with the big threat of 29 Nxg6+! hxg6 30 Qh4+ Kg8 31 Rxg7+! Kxg7 32 Qxf6+ and mates, while if 28...Rf8 29 Nxd5 Qxd5 (29...exd5? 30 Qe7 Rg8 runs into 31 Qxg7+! Rxg7 32 Rc8+ Rg8 33 Bxf6 mate) 30 Rc5 Qd6 31 Rxc4 Qxf4 32 b3 leaves White is in control.

27 Nc8! (Diagram 49)

A pretty move, threatening both Qd8+ and Nd6.

27...Qd5 28 Nd6

Now the knight hits both f7 and c4.

28...Kg8 29 Nxc4!

A better pawn to take than f7, as White now has a passed c-pawn and has taken away the d3 outpost which Black could otherwise have used for his light-squared bishop.

29...Rb8 30 Qxd5 exd5

Or 30...Bxd5 31 Nxa5 and White should convert his material advantage, since 31...Rxb2?! loses to 32 Rc8+ Bf8 33 Bc5.

31 Ba7!

Forcing the rook off the b-file (31...Rb5? loses straight away to 32 a4 Rb3 33 Rc8+ Bf8 34 Nxa5 Rxb2 35 Bc5), thereby keeping the b2-pawn safe. If 31 Nxa5?! then 31...d4! muddies the waters.

31...Ra8 32 Nd6

Again 32 Nxa5 d4! is unduly complicated, and 33 cxd4? actually loses to 33...Rxa7! 34 Rxa7 Bxd4+.

32...Bb1 33 Nxf7 Bxa2 34 Ng5 Re8 35 Bd4 (Diagram 50) 35...Bh6?

Diagram 49 (B)

Threatening both Qd8+ and Nd6

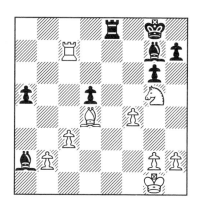

Diagram 50 (B)

White is winning

Black blunders but his position was lost anyway: a pawn down with his bishop on a2 outclassed by the white knight.

36 Nxh7 Re6 37 g3 1-0

There is no defence to Nf6+.

Conclusion

5 Bb5 Nd4 is the main line of the whole Grand Prix Attack. White cedes the two bishops but gains space and a lead in development. I think 6 0-0 is the only way to fight for an advantage, though White has options after 6...Nxb5 7 Nxb5 d5, either taking the pawn on d5 or else playing 8 e5. The critical variation after 8 exd5 is probably 8...a6 9 Nc3 Nf6 10 d4 c4 which leaves an interesting position: Black has the two bishops and more space on the queenside; on the other hand, White has a temporary material and development advantage and can try and exploit that, either by retaining the pawn or by generating some initiative. 8 e5 is less explored and normally develops into positions where Black has to be careful not to be worse with less space and his bishop on g7 blocked out of the game.

Chapter Three

2...d6 3 f4

▨ **The First Few Moves**

▨ **Illustrative Games**

▨ **Conclusion**

The First Few Moves

1 e4 c5 2 Nc3 d6

2...d6 is the move you should be happiest to play against out of all Black's main options. The Grand Prix Attack works best against 2...d6 and has been played by the world's top players including the new World Champion, Vishy Anand. White's plan is f2-f4, Nf3, Bc4, castle kingside and launch a quick offensive against the black king. As Black has already played 2...d6, the break ...d5 is less attractive.

It might seem strange that anyone goes for 2...d6, when 2...Nc6 or 2...e6 are stronger options against the Grand Prix Attack. However, Black may feel obliged to play it, in case White decides to open the Sicilian with d2-d4 after all. For instance, 2...Nc6 3 Nge2 and 4 d4, or 2...e6 3 Nf3 and 4 d4, circumvents certain mainline Sicilians such as the Najdorf, which may be Black's defence of choice.

3 f4 g6

Lines where Black plays an early ...a7-a6 will be examined in Chapter Five.

4 Nf3 Bg7 (Diagram 1)

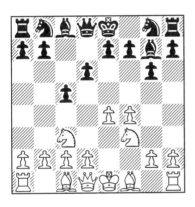

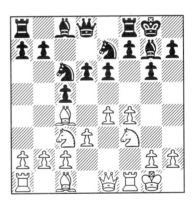

Diagram 1 (W)	Diagram 2 (W)
Black plays ...d6	A standard Grand Prix set-up

5 Bc4

5 Bb5+!? is another very interesting idea suggested in *Chess Openings for White, Explained*. If 5...Nc6 then 6 Bxc6+ bxc6 7 d3 transposes to 3 Bb5 variations without 3...Nd4 which are very comfortable for White (see Chapter Six), while after 5...Bd7 6 Bc4! we have a position similar to the main line but with the black bishop on d7. This probably favours White as the pawn break ...d6-d5 is now harder to construct, ...Qd4+ is no longer possible for Black in some positions, and once Black plays ...e7-e6 the pawn on d6 won't be protected.

5...Nc6 6 0-0 e6

As we have already seen in Chapter One, ...e7-e6 and ...Nge7 is the standard set-up against White's Bc4. Otherwise Black mostly plays 6...Nf6, and this is examined in Game 16.

7 d3

The impetuous 7 f5?! featured in the game Hellers-Gelfand, in the Introduction.

7...Nge7 8 Qe1 0-0 (Diagram 2)

The most logical continuation, although it allows White a quick attack on the kingside. Other moves will be examined in Game 15. After the text White can go straight for the kill with 9 f5!? as in the first game below, while the safer 9 a3 is the subject of Game 14.

Statistics

White has scored well in this line with 57%, including 1676 wins and just 1146 losses out of the 3689 games in my database. However, things have not been so promising for White recently. In the past few years, between players above 2300, White has scored just 42% with 28 wins and 48 losses out of 133 games in my database. This is probably due to Black's recent discovery of 9...gxf5 which appears to make 8...0-0 playable. Nevertheless, I believe White can still obtain good positions in this line.

Illustrative Games

Game 13
☐ **N.Short** ■ **L.Oll**
Tallinn 1998

1 e4 c5 2 Nc3 d6 3 f4 Nc6 4 Nf3 g6 5 Bc4

In the 2...Nc6 lines, 5 Bc4 is not so effective as it encourages Black to play a quick ...e7-e6 and ...d7-d5, gaining time on the bishop. Here, however, Black has already committed his d-pawn and so the plan of ...e6 and ...d5 is a tempo slower.

5...Bg7 6 0-0 e6 7 d3 Nge7 8 Qe1!

Indirectly preventing the freeing break ...d6-d5.

> **NOTE: Pieces can be 'pinned' even when there are more pieces on the file.**

8...0-0 9 f5!? (Diagram 3)

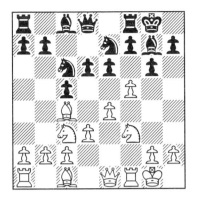

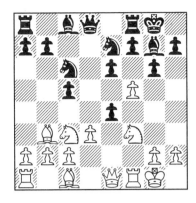

Diagram 3 (B)

White attacks straight away

Diagram 4 (W)

Black accepts the pawn

White attacks instantly trying to break through. If Black does not do something quickly White will play Qh4, Bh6 and Ng5 with a decisive attack. A more restrained alternative, 9 a3, is examined in the next game.

9...d5

After 9...exf5 10 Qh4! Black is already in trouble as White's attack is far too strong; e.g. 10...Qc7 (10...Ne5 11 Bg5! wins a piece) 11 Bh6 Ne5 12 Ng5 Nxc4 13 Bxg7 Kxg7 14 Qxh7+ Kf6 15 e5+! and mates, as given by Bangiev.

The other capture, 9...gxf5, is a brave move which has been played by the young Ukrainian GM Sergey Karjakin. With accurate defence it seems Black can hold, so this must be his best try. Nevertheless, White has plenty of play for the pawn and I wouldn't worry about playing this position against anyone below 2600! For example, 10 Qg3!? (10 Qh4 is also possible) 10...fxe4 11 dxe4 Ng6 12 h4?! (an interesting try, but probably not sound; instead 12 Be3 or 12 Bg5!? f6 13 Be3 leaves White with good compensation for the pawn) 12...Nce5! 13 Bg5 Qb6! (rather than 13...f6 14 Nxe5 Nxe5 15 Bh6 as in B.Macieja-L.Dominguez, Bled Olympiad 2002) 14 Nxe5 Bxe5 and Black has fought off the worst of the attack.

10 Bb3

Obviously White keeps the tension in the centre, as taking on d5 would help Black out immensely.

10...c4

Blocking in White's bishop on b3. 10...gxf5 is less effective now: 11 exd5 exd5 12 Qh4 with excellent compensation. The main alternative is 10...dxe4 **(Diagram 4)** and then:

a) 11 dxe4 exf5 (11...gxf5 might also be playable) 12 Qh4 gives White a pleasant initiative for the pawn, but Black can trade queens after 12...fxe4 13 Nxe4 Nf5! (not 13...b6? 14 Nfg5) 14 Qxd8 Rxd8 15 Nxc5 for a roughly level position. If instead 13 Ng5!?, then 13...h6! and White is the player having to be careful; e.g. 14 Nxf7 Qd4+ 15 Kh1 c4 16 Nxh6+ Bxh6 17 Bxh6 Rxf1+ 18 Rxf1 Nf5 19 Qg5 (19 Qg4? was just losing after 19...Ne5 20 Qf4 cxb3 in B.Macieja-H.Nakamura, Bermuda 2002) 19...Kh7 20 Rd1, when Black can force a draw by 20...Qe5 21 Nd5 Nxh6 22 Nf6+ Kg7 23 Nh5+ etc, or try for more with 20...Qxd1+! 21 Nxd1 cxb3 22 axb3 Nxh6.

b) 11 f6!? exf3 (11...Bxf6 12 Nxe4 Bg7 13 Nxc5 is slightly better for White, who can also try 13 Bg5 with a good attack for the pawn while Black still has problems completing his development) 12 fxg7 Kxg7 13 Rxf3, R.Polzin-A.Huzman, European Club Cup, Chalkidiki 2002, leads to an unclear position where White probably holds the upper hand with the two bishops, open lines, faster development and the prospect of a quick attack against the black king, especially as Black has lost the defensive abilities of his dark-squared bishop. All this play should be worth the sacrificed pawn.

11 dxc4 d4

11...dxe4 12 f6! is a clever intermezzo, giving up the f-pawn on White's own terms and not allowing Black time to consolidate his pawn structure. After 12...Bxf6 (or 12...exf3 13 fxg7 Kxg7 14 Rxf3) 13 Nxe4 Bg7 14 c5 Qc7 15 Qh4, White was clearly better in Z.Hracek-M.Wahls, German League 1996.

12 f6! (Diagram 5)

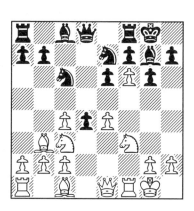 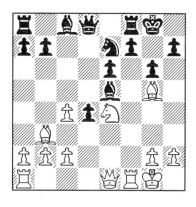

Diagram 5 (B)

A thematic advance

Diagram 6 (B)

Playing on the dark squares

Short uses the same idea as in the previous note. White gains time on Black's dark-squared bishop to get his knight to the useful e4-square.

12...Bxf6 13 e5!

The point of 12 f6.

13...Bg7

If 13...Bxe5 14 Nxe5 dxc3 15 Qxc3 Nxe5 16 Qxe5 Nf5 17 Bf4 (either 17 c3 or 17 Be3!? keeps the queens on) 17...f6 18 Qc3 Qd4+ 19 Qxd4 Nxd4 20 Bh6 Nxb3 and now 21 axb3 Rf7 22 Rad1 maintains the initiative, whereas 21 Rad1?! Na5 22 Bxf8 Kxf8 23 Rxf6+ Ke7 24 Rdf1 Nxc4 25 Rf7+ Kd6 26 Rxh7 b5 led to a draw in A.Khalifman-V.Savon, Moscow 1992.

14 Ne4

14 Nb5 has also been played but doesn't seem as natural as 14 Ne4.

14...Nxe5

14...h6 15 Nf6+ Kh8 (15...Bxf6 16 exf6 Nf5 17 Ne5 leaves White with a huge initiative) 16 g4!? (not allowing Black the use of the f5-square for his knight) 16...Ng8 17 g5 with a deadly attack.

15 Nxe5 Bxe5 16 Bg5 (Diagram 6)

Controlling the f6-square. White threatens Nf6+ when he would have a mating net around the enemy king, so Black's reply is almost forced.

16...f5

16...Qc7 17 Nf6+ Bxf6 (17...Kg7? loses at once to 18 Bh6+!) 18 Bxf6 Nf5 is the way *Fritz* wants to play, but I don't know any humans who would want to defend this position, as the bishop on f6 means that Black must be very careful for the rest of the game. Notably *Fritz* evaluates this position as better for White despite the pawn deficit.

17 Qh4! Rf7 18 Nf6+

Forcing Black to swap off his dark-squared bishop, leaving him with a weak kingside, and winning back the pawn into the bargain.

18...Bxf6

18...Kh8 19 Rae1 is awful for Black, e.g. 19...Qa5 (or 19...Bd6 20 Ng4! Rg7 21 Ne5) 20 Ng4! and White is winning. N.Mitkov-H.Stefansson, Hartberg 1991, concluded 20...Bg7 21 Bxe7 Qc7 22 Bd8 Qc5 23 Nf6 h6 24 Ne4 Qf8 25 Ng5 Rf6 26 c5 Bd7 27 Bc7 Qxc5 28 Be5 1-0.

19 Bxf6 Qf8

If 19...Rxf6 20 Qxf6 Nc6 21 Qxd8+ Nxd8 22 Rad1 Nc6 23 Ba4 e5 24 Rfe1 e4 25 Bxc6 bxc6 26 Rxd4 with a decisive advantage.

20 Bxd4 Nc6 21 Be3

Keeping an eye on both the c5 and h6-squares. 21 Bc3!? is also possible.

21...Qe7

21...b6 22 c5! bxc5 23 Qc4 Nd4 24 Bxd4 cxd4 25 Qxd4 is a line given by Short in his annotations, and indeed leaves White with a clear edge.

22 Qxe7 Rxe7 (Diagram 7)

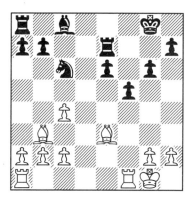

Diagram 7 (W)	Diagram 8 (B)
Black still has problems	Swapping off to win

Black has managed to weather the attack a little by swapping off queens, but still has problems due to his lack of development, weak kingside and White's two bishops.

23 c5

23 Bg5 would have been better according to Short, who analyses 23...Re8 (or 23...Rf7 24 Rad1 Bd7 25 c5 Re8 26 a3) 24 Rad1 e5 25 c5+ Be6 26 Rd7 with a clear advantage, e.g. 26...Bxb3 27 axb3 b6 28 Bf6 bxc5 29 Rfd1.

23...Kg7?

23...Na5, attempting to swap off White's b3-bishop, would have been a better attempt to hold. White is still better with something like 24 Bf4, but the opposite-coloured bishop ending might prove tricky to win after 24...Nxb3 25 axb3 e5 26 Rfe1 e4.

24 Bg5 Re8 25 Rad1 h6 26 Bd2!

Bringing the bishop round to the c3-square.

26...e5 27 Bc3 Be6

Black sacrifices a pawn to finally develop his queenside, but Short comfortably converts White's material advantage.

28 Bxe6 Rxe6 29 Rd7+ Re7 30 Rxe7+ Nxe7 31 Bxe5+ Kf7 32 Rd1 Nc6 33 Bc7 Re8 34 Kf2 Re7 35 Bd6 Re4 36 c3 a5 37 b3 a4 38 Bc7! Re7 39 Bb6 axb3 40 axb3 f4 41 b4 Ne5 42 Bd8! Re8 43 Bc7 (Diagram 8)

Swapping off the minor pieces as the rook ending is much easier to win.

TIP: When material up, try to avoid any imbalances as they give the defending side additional chances.

43...Kf6 44 Bxe5+ Rxe5 45 Rd7

Black has no chances of holding anymore as White's queenside pawns are too strong.

45...Re3 46 c4 Rc3 47 Rxb7 Rxc4 48 Ke2! Rc2+ 49 Kd3 Rxg2 50 c6 Ke6 51 b5 f3 52 c7 Kd7 53 b6 1-0

Game 14
☐ **M.Chandler** ■ **A.Schenk**
British League 2006

---

1 e4 c5 2 Nc3 d6 3 f4 g6 4 Nf3 Bg7 5 Bc4 Nc6 6 0-0 e6 7 d3 Nge7 8 Qe1 0-0 9 a3 (Diagram 9)

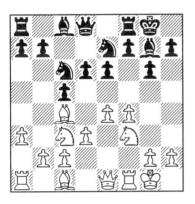

Diagram 9 (B)	Diagram 10 (B)
Giving the bishop a retreat	White begins the attack

A safer move than 9 f5!? which we looked at in the previous game. White makes ready to drop the bishop back to a2, rather than b3 when he would have to be alert to the threat of ...c5-c4 after either ...b7-b5 or ...Qb6.

9...Nd4

9...d5 might be a better try for Black, e.g. 10 Bb3 (a little odd given White's previous move, and indeed Black's play revolves around the bishop's exposure on b3) 10...Nd4 11 Nxd4 cxd4 12 Ne2 dxe4 13 dxe4 d3 14 Nc3 (not 14 cxd3? Qb6+) 14...Nc6 15 Be3 Nd4 16 Bxd4 Qxd4+ 17 Kh1 Qb6 18 Na4 Qb5 19 Nc3 Qb6 20 Na4 Qb5 21 Nc3 ½-½ E.Sutovsky-M.Palac, Saint Vincent 2002.

10 Qf2 Nxf3+ 11 Qxf3 Bd7 12 Be3 a6 13 Ba2 b5 14 Rae1 a5

White has all his pieces pointing towards the black king and can now start the attack. 14...b4!? 15 axb4 cxb4 16 Nd1 Qc7 offered better chances to equalize.

15 f5! (Diagram 10) 15...Nc6?

Black has to take the pawn, but White still generates a strong attack:

a) 15...exf5 16 Bg5! (threatening exf5) 16...h6 17 Bxe7 Qxe7 18 exf5 Qf6 19 fxg6 Qxg6 20 Nd5 with a clear advantage.

b) 15...gxf5 16 Qg3! (with ideas of Bh6 or Qxd6) 16...b4 (not 16...Qc7? 17 exf5 Nxf5 18 Rxf5! exf5 19 Bh6 or 17...exf5 18 Nd5! and wins) 17 Bh6 Ng6 18 Bxg7 Kxg7 (if 18...f4 19 Rxf4 Kxg7 20 Nd1 and White can continue his attack without any material deficit) 19 exf5 exf5 20 Nd5 gives White huge compensation for the pawn: Black's kingside has been shattered, White has a nice outpost for his knight on d5, his bishop on a2 has an open diagonal towards the black king, and his rooks are centralized and ready to attack.

16 f6!

The pawn on f6 cuts out Black's strong g7-bishop as well as continuing the attack.

16...Bh8 17 Qf4 b4 18 Nd1

Not 18 axb4? axb4 when White loses a piece, but perhaps 18 Nb5 is more accurate, attacking d6 while retaining mate threats.

18...Ne5 19 Qh4 Bb5 20 Bh6 Re8 21 Re3 (Diagram 11)

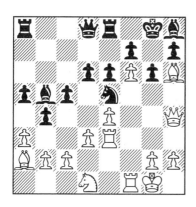

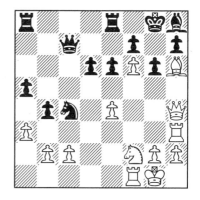

Diagram 11 (B)

Planning mate down the h-file

Diagram 12 (B)

Preparing the final assault

White's idea is crude but effective: to play Rh3, move the h6-bishop out of the way and mate. Black does not have a satisfactory way of stopping this.

21...c4 22 dxc4 Bxc4 23 Bxc4 Nxc4 24 Rh3 Qc7 25 Nf2! (Diagram 12)

Bringing the offside knight into play, defending the e4-pawn, and eliminating queen checks on the a7-g1 diagonal. The immediate 25 Bg7? h5 26 Qg5? would allow 26...Bxg7 27 fxg7 Qc5+! and White's attack is over.

25...Rab8

If 25...Qc5 26 Be3! wins.

26 Bg7! h5

Of course 26...Bxg7? gets mated after 27 Qxh7+ Kf8 28 Qxg7.

27 Bxh8 Rb5

Desperation, since White is now a piece up and still attacking, but if 27...Kxh8 28 Qg5 Kh7 29 Rxh5+! and mates.

28 Bg7 Nxb2 29 Qf4 1-0

Game 15
☐ V.Anand ▉ B.Gelfand
Wijk aan Zee 1996

In this game between two super-GMs, Anand (currently rated number one in the world) won very quickly with the white pieces, which shows how hard the Grand Prix is to combat.

1 e4 c5 2 Nc3 d6 3 f4 g6 4 Nf3 Bg7 5 Bc4 Nc6 6 d3 e6 7 0-0 Nge7 8 Qe1 h6 (Diagram 13)

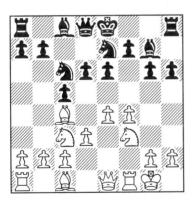
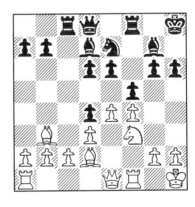

Diagram 13 (W)
Black delays ...0-0

Diagram 14 (W)
Decision time for White

This used to be considered almost forced since 8...0-0 allows White a massive attack, as we have seen.

Another idea is 8...Nd4, but after 9 Nxd4 cxd4 10 Ne2 Black lacks counterplay and must be careful the d4-pawn doesn't just drop off. N.Short-B.Gelfand, 3rd match-game, Brussels 1991, continued 10...0-0 (if 10...d5 at once then 11 Bb5+ Bd7 12 Bxd7+ Qxd7 13 e5 cuts off the d4-pawn) 11 Bb3! (to be able to answer ...d6-d5 with e4-e5) 11...Nc6 12 Bd2 (preventing ...Na5) 12...d5 13 e5 f6 14 exf6 Bxf6 15 Kh1!, preparing the familiar manoeuvre Ne2-g1-f3, and White was clearly better.

9 Bb3

Dropping the bishop back so that ...d6-d5 won't come with tempo. As Black has not yet committed his king, White merely improves the positioning of his pieces while he waits to see what Black will do. 9 Bd2, as in J.Gdanski-R.Kuczynski, Polish Championship, Warsaw 2001, is another option, completing White's development. However, Bb3 (or else a3/a4 and Ba2) will almost certainly have to be played at some point, while d2 might not be the best square for the other bishop.

9...a6

Black also tries to improve his position while continuing to delay castling. Various other ideas have been seen here:

a) 9...0-0?! makes no sense as the inclusion of Bb3 and ...h7-h6 has clearly favoured White, so the f4-f5 break will be even stronger: 10 f5! exf5 (10...gxf5 11 Qh4 Ng6 12 Qh5 f4 13 Ne2 Qf6 14 c3 is also very unpleasant for Black) 11 Qh4 with a clear advantage, e.g. 11...g5 12 Bxg5! hxg5 13 Nxg5 Re8 14 Bxf7+ Kf8 15 Be6! threatens Nh7 mate so Black is forced to give up his queen (15...Bxe6 16 Nxe6+ and 17 Nxd8).

b) 9...Rb8 10 Be3 0-0 (if 10...b5 then 11 e5) 11 Rd1 (intending to break with d3-d4) 11...Nd4 12 Bxd4!? cxd4 13 Ne2 Nc6 14 Qf2 Qb6 and now, instead of 15 Ng3 (D.Reinderman-V.Gurevich, German League 2001), 15 c3! dxc3 16 Qxb6 axb6 17 bxc3 would give White an edge in the queenless middlegame; and 15 g4!? is another possibility.

c) 9...Nd4 seems logical as Black wants to alleviate his slightly more cramped position, while White's attack will be diminished with fewer pieces. However, Black faces the same problems as before after 10 Nxd4 cxd4 11 Ne2 0-0 12 Kh1! (once again with the idea of bringing the knight round to f3 via g1) 12...f5 (not wanting to allow White any more time to play f4-f5, Black plays it himself, ensuring his king will be slightly safer but also weakening his pawn structure) 13 Ng1 Kh8 14 Nf3 Bd7 15 Bd2 Rc8 **(Diagram 14)** was V.Topalov-L.Van Wely, Wijk aan Zee 1996. White has completed his development and now must look at how to proceed. In the game 16 Qg3 fxe4 17 dxe4 d5 18 exd5 exd5 was rather unclear, but 16 e5! would give White a clear advantage. After 16...dxe5 17 Nxe5! (threatening to win the exchange and a pawn with Nxd7) 17...Be8 18 Qg3 Kh7 19 Rae1 White has a very pleasant position. All his pieces are on their optimum squares – in particular, the knight on e5 controls the whole board – whereas Black's pieces are passive and he is struggling to hold on to his pawns.

10 e5!? (Diagram 15)

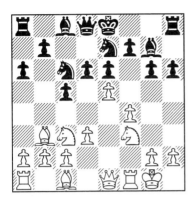

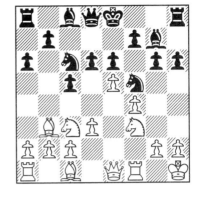

Diagram 15 (B)
An alternative pawn break

Diagram 16 (B)
Making the king secure

A slightly unusual pawn break. As we have seen, White normally plays for f4-f5, but that does not have the same force with Black having delayed castling. Instead White plays more positionally, blocking in the bishop on g7.

More recently 10 a4 was tried by GM Emil Sutovsky in a very interesting game: 10...Rb8 11 Be3 b6?! (11...0-0 is probably better as the immediate f4-f5 does not have as much punch: 12 f5?! gxf5! 13 Qh4 Ng6 14 Qh5 f4 and Black gains time on the bishop to consolidate; instead White should play 12 Qh4 and then look to follow with f4-f5) 12 Qh4 Na5 13 Ba2 Nec6 14 Qg3! Nb4 15 f5! Nxa2 (15...Nxc2 16 fxe6 Nxe3 17 exf7+ is extremely dangerous for Black) 16 Nxa2 exf5 17 exf5 Bxf5 18 Nh4 Be5 (18...Be6 runs into 19 Nxg6!) 19 Bf4! Bxf4?! (but if 19...Qf6 20 Rae1 Nc6 21 Nf3 regains the pawn with a clear advantage) 20 Qxf4 Be6 21 Nxg6!! fxg6 22 Rae1 Qe7 (if 22...Kd7 23 Rxe6 Kxe6 24 Qf7+ mates) 23 Nc3 Kd7 24 Nd5 Bxd5 25 Rxe7+ Kxe7 26 b4! Nc6 27 Qf6+ Kd7 28 c4 Nxb4 29 cxd5 Nxd5 30 Qxg6 and White eventually won in E.Sutovsky-B.Gelfand, Israeli Team Championship 2000. Black has rook, knight and pawn for the queen, but his king is exposed and his pawns will start to drop.

10...Nf5

It looks too dangerous to win the pawn with 10...dxe5 11 fxe5 Nxe5 (or 11...g5 12 Ne4) 12 Nxe5 Qd4+ 13 Kh1 (not 13 Be3?! as Black has a trick in 13...Qxe5 14 Qf2 Qe3! 15 Qxe3 Bd4) 13...Qxe5 14 Ne4, when the threats of Bf4 and Qf2 leave Black in deep trouble; e.g. 14...0-0?! (14...Qc7 15 Bf4 e5 16 Bxf7+!) 15 Bf4 Qh5 16 Bd6, or 15 Bxh6!? as 15...Bxh6?? drops the queen to 16 Nf6+.

10...d5 seems the most natural move, but g7 is not the best square for the dark-squared bishop in this French-type pawn structure, while the c8-bishop is also blocked in. 11 Ne2 0-0 12 c3 Bd7 13 Qf2 b6 14 d4 gives White a comfortable edge.

11 Kh1! (Diagram 16)

Sidestepping to rule out any checks from d4, which might yet prove troublesome after Black captures on e5.

11...Nfd4

11...0-0 is still better for White after 12 Ne4. Instead, 11...d5 is a slightly improved version of 10...d5 for Black. A.Khalifman-L.Van Wely, European Cup Final, Bugojno 1999, continued 12 Ne2 h5 13 c3 b6 14 Ng3 Nce7 15 Nxf5 Nxf5 16 d4 a5 17 Ba4+ Bd7 18 Bc2 Bb5 19 Rf2 Bf8 20 Be3 Rc8 21 Rd1 Be7 22 Rfd2 cxd4 23 Nxd4 Nxd4 and the players agreed a draw.

Van Wely also suggests 11...Ncd4!?, one point being that 12 Ne4 Nxf3 13 Rxf3 dxe5 14 fxe5 (as in the game) and then 14...Bxe5 is more appealing for Black since the f5-knight covers d6, i.e. after 15 Bf4 Bxb2.

12 Ne4

After 12 Nxd4 cxd4 13 Ne4 dxe5 it looks like Black has about enough to hold equality; e.g. 14 Qg3 (14 fxe5 Bxe5) 14...Qe7 15 fxe5 Bxe5 16 Bf4 Bxf4 17 Rxf4 17...f5! (but not 17...0-0 18 Rf6!) 18 Qxg6+ Kd8 19 Ng3 Qg5! 20 Qf7 Qe7 with equality is a line given by Anand. White might try 17 Qxf4!? f5 18 Nd6+ Kd8 19 Qg3 with the initiative, but 12 Ne4 keeps more tension in the position.

12...Nxf3

12...dxe5 13 Nxe5! is clearly better for White.

13 Rxf3

Obviously not 13 Nxd6+? Qxd6! winning a piece.

13...dxe5 14 fxe5 Nxe5

On 14...Bxe5 15 Bf4! swaps off Black's important dark-squared bishop (15...Bxb2 now walks into 16 Nd6+ Kf8 17 Nxf7!), leaving numerous weaknesses in his position, in particular the hole on f6, and guarantees White the advantage.

15 Rf1 (Diagram 17)

Calmly dropping the rook back. Black has an extra pawn but his king is vulnerable, while White's knight is strong on e4, hitting the c5-pawn and looking to drop into either d6 or f6. White will develop his pieces very swiftly to useful squares and he has plenty of compensation for the pawn.

15...g5

Forced, according to Anand, but this leaves White with a clear advantage. The problem for Black is that he cannot castle due to 15...0-0 16 Bxh6! Bxh6 17 Nf6+, and otherwise the strong 16 Bf4 is coming; e.g. 15...Qe7 16 Bf4, threatening 17 Qg3 against any Black move (even 16...g5 or 16...f5), or 15...b6 16 Bf4 and it's doubtful that Black will survive the attack.

16 Qg3

Reinstating the threat of Bf4, perhaps with the further idea of h2-h4 to open the kingside. If Black counters these moves (e.g. with 16...f5) then White may simply take on c5, when he is no longer even a pawn down.

16...0-0 17 Bxg5!?

An interesting piece sacrifice which breaks up Black's kingside and leaves him needing to find 'only moves' to survive. Instead, 17 Nxc5 would allow Black to develop his final pieces and reach approximate equality with 17...b6 18 Ne4 f5. However, the best move might be 17 Bd2!?, with the simple idea of swapping off the dark-squared bishops with Bc3, when Black will have a lot of holes around his king; e.g. 17...Ng6 18 Bc3 b6 19 Bf6 Bxf6 20 Nxf6+ and White has easily enough compensation for the pawn.

17...hxg5 18 Nxg5

White threatens 19 Qh4 (e.g. 18...b5 19 Qh4 Re8 20 Rae1! c4 21 Rxe5 Bxe5 22 Qh7+ Kf8 23 Qxf7 mate), so Black's reply is forced.

18...Ng6 19 Rae1! (Diagram 18)

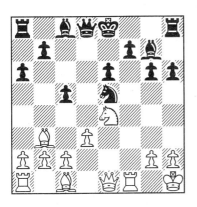

Diagram 17 (B)

White has good compensation

Diagram 18 (B)

Accurate defence is needed

Bringing the last piece into the attack. The position is dynamically balanced now, and with perfect play Black should be fine, but any slight slip will grant White a swift victory.

19...Qe7

Black has several other possibilities:

a) 19...Bh6? loses at once to 20 Nxf7! Rxf7 21 Qxg6+.

b) 19...Bxb2 looks a bit greedy and White has at least a draw after 20 Nxf7! (better than 20 Nxe6 fxe6 21 Qxg6+ Bg7 22 Bxe6+ Bxe6 23 Qxe6+ Kh7) 20...Rxf7 21 Qxg6+

Rg7 22 Bxe6+ Bxe6 23 Qxe6+ Kh8 24 Re3 Rh7 25 Rf7 as given by Anand, when White retains the attack with two pawns for the piece.

c) 19...Bf6 20 Rxe6!? (otherwise 20 Nxe6 fxe6 21 Qxg6+ Bg7 22 Bxe6+ Bxe6 23 Qxe6+ Kh7 is the line above with an extra pawn for White) 20...Bxe6 (not 20...Bxg5? 21 Rxg6+ or 20...fxe6 21 Nxe6 and wins) 21 Nxe6 Qe7! reaches a very complex position where 22 Nf4 looks best, and Black probably has to return a piece to survive; i.e. after 22...Kh8 (not 22...Kg7? 23 Nh5+) 23 Qh3+ Bh4 24 g3.

20 Rf5!! (Diagram 19)

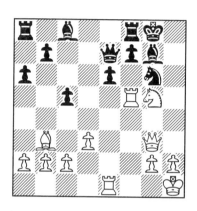

Diagram 19 (B)

A very aesthetic move

Diagram 20 (B)

White is winning

A very visual move. White wants to defend the knight on g5 so he can move his queen to h3, while 20...exf5? loses quickly after 21 Rxe7 Nxe7 22 Qh4 Rd8 23 Qh5!.

20...Bf6

The alternative was 20...Bh6 21 Nxf7 (Anand's idea of 21 h4!? followed by h4-h5 also looks strong for White) and then:

a) 21...Rxf7 22 Qxg6+ Bg7 23 Rxe6 Bxe6 24 Bxe6 Raf8 25 Rg5! (threatening Qxg7 mate) 25...Kh8 (not 25...Qf6? 26 Qxf6!) 26 Rh5+ Bh6 27 Rxh6+ Rh7 28 Kg1 Qg7 29 Rxh7+ Qxh7 30 Qg5 is clearly better for White with three pawns for the exchange.

b) 21...Kg7 22 Ne5 Rf6 (if 22...Rxf5 23 Qxg6+ Kf8 24 Qxf5+! exf5 25 Nxg6+ wins, or similarly 23...Kh8 24 Qxf5!) 23 Rf3! should be winning for White as he is threatening Ref1.

c) 21...Kh7! 22 Nxh6 Kxh6 23 Qe3+ Kg7 24 Rxc5 when White has three pawns for the piece, still with attacking prospects.

21 Nxe6

21 h4!? should again be considered, but perhaps 21...e5! is good for Black.

21...fxe6??

The pressure on Gelfand to find the only move is too much and he gifts White the victory. 21...Re8! was forced, when Anand considers that White should have enough compensation after 22 Re4 or 22 Rff1!?.

22 Rxe6!

Not 22 Qxg6+? Qg7 23 Rxe6? Qxg6 24 Ref6+ Kh7! and Black wins. But by playing 22 Rxe6 first White eliminates this defence.

22...Kg7

Now if 22...Bxe6 23 Qxg6+ Qg7 24 Bxe6+ Rf7 (or 24...Kh8 25 Rh5+ and mates) 25 Bxf7+ Kf8 26 Qxf6 wins.

23 Rxe7+ Bxe7 24 Rxf8 Bxf8 25 h4! (Diagram 20) 1-0

Black has rook, bishop and knight for queen and three pawns, but his king is still far too exposed, three of his pieces are on their starting squares and he has no way to retain his material. So Gelfand resigned; a sample line might run 25...Kh7 26 Qf3! Bg7 27 Bf7! Nf8 28 Qh5+ Bh6 29 g4 Be6 30 Bxe6 Nxe6 31 g5 and White wins.

Game 16
□ **N.Mitkov** ■ **Joh.Alvarez**
Istanbul Olympiad 2000

1 e4 c5 2 Nc3 d6 3 f4 Nc6 4 Nf3 g6 5 Bc4 Bg7 6 0-0 Nf6 (Diagram 21)

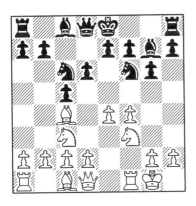
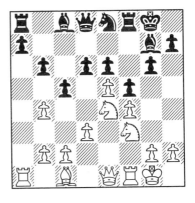

Diagram 21 (W)
Black plays ...Nf6

Diagram 22 (W)
Fighting on the dark squares

An alternative scheme of development to the usual ...e7-e6 and ...Nge7.

7 d3

I played 7 Qe1 in G.Jones-V.Kuzubov, Groningen 2004, and after 7...0-0 8 f5!? Nd4 9 fxg6 Nxf3+ (9...Nxc2 is too risky: 10 Qh4 Nxa1 11 Ng5 e6 12 Rxf6 h6 13 gxf7+ Rxf7 14 Rxf7 Qxg5 15 Qxg5 hxg5 16 Rc7 is a long forcing line which leaves White with a clear edge) 10 Rxf3 hxg6 11 Qh4 e6 12 d3 Nh7 13 Qg3 d5 14 exd5 exd5 15 Bxd5!? Bxc3 16 Qxg6+ Kh8 17 Bxf7 Bd4+ 18 Kh1 Qb6 19 Qh5 Be6 20 Bg6 Bg8 21 Bf4 Qe6 22 Raf1 Bg7 23 Be4 Rf6 24 Rh3 Raf8 25 Bxh7 Rh6, now 26 Be4! would have left me with a winning advantage after 26...Rxh5 27 Rxh5+ Bh7 28 Rxh7+ Kg8 29 Rh5. However, 7...Nb4! thwarts this idea as White has nothing better than 8 Qd1, when Black (if he wants) can repeat the position with 8...Nc6.

7...0-0 8 Qe1

8 f5 looks promising, but unfortunately Black has 8...e6! which seems to hold the balance. Instead, 8 Bb3 will probably transpose to note 'd' to Black's next move (i.e. after 8...Na5 9 Qe1 Nxb3 10 axb3). Otherwise 8...Nd4 (8...a6?! 9 Qe1 Na5 10 f5 Nxb3 11 axb3 is similar to that game) 9 Nxd4 (better than 9 Qe1 a5!, as in Gil.Hernandez-V.Anand, Merida 2001, when the bishop on b3 is in danger of being trapped) 9...cxd4 10 Ne2 promises White a pleasant game, since Black does not have ...d6-d5 at his disposal (as he would if the bishop were still on c4); for example, 10...Nd7 11 Qe1 Nc5 12 Qf2 Qb6 13 f5 Nxb3 14 axb3 d5 15 Bg5 dxe4 16 dxe4 f6 17 Bh4 e5 18 fxe6 Qxe6 19 Nxd4 Qxe4 20 Rfe1 Qd5 21 c4 Qc5 22 Nb5 Qxf2+ 23 Bxf2 was clearly better for White in M.Al Modiahki-Joh.Alvarez, Istanbul Olympiad 2000.

8...a6?!

As White is going to drop the bishop back to b3 in any case, this move just wastes a vital tempo. Black has tried several other moves, of which 8...Nd4 and 8...Na5 are critical.

a) 8...Bg4?! 9 e5! Ne8 10 Ng5 dxe5 11 Qh4 h5 12 h3 Bc8 13 f5 Bxf5 14 Rxf5! Qd4+? (but if 14...gxf5 15 Qxh5 Nf6 16 Bxf7+ Rxf7 17 Qxf7+ Kh8 18 Qg6 Qe8 19 Qxf5 leaves White a pawn up) 15 Qxd4 exd4 16 Rxf7 1-0 B.Macieja-Joh.Alvarez, Bermuda 2001 (as already seen in the book's introduction).

b) 8...e6 9 Bb3 Na5 10 e5! (the typical response to ...e7-e6) 10...Ne8 11 Bd2 Nxb3 12 axb3 d5 13 d4 b6 14 Be3 c4 15 bxc4 dxc4 16 Qe2 Bb7 17 Qxc4 and White went on to win in L.Fressinet-M.Sebag, Paris 2004.

c) 8...Nd4 9 Nxd4 cxd4 10 Nd5 (if 10 Ne2 d5! is effective as White can't push past with e4-e5) 10...Nxd5 11 exd5!? (11 Bxd5 Qc7 12 f5 e6! is rather unclear) 11...f5?! (ambitious, but this creates weaknesses in Black's camp and hems in the bishop on c8) 12 a4 a6 13 b4 Bd7 14 Bb2 Rc8 15 a5 Bb5 16 Bb3 Kh8 17 Qf2 won material in B.Macieja-E.Pähtz, Internet (blitz) 2004.

d) 8...Na5!? 9 Bb3 Nxb3 (9...e6 transposes to note 'b') 10 axb3 (Black has the two bishops but has to be very careful to stop White's thematic plan of Qh4, f4-f5, Bh6 and Ng5) 10...e6 (if 10...Ne8 then 11 f5!?) 11 e5 (trying to exploit the weakening of the d6-square) 11...Ne8 12 Ne4 b6 13 b4 f5 **(Diagram 22)** was S.Kudrin-N.De Fir-

nian, US Championship, Denver 1998, and now 14 Neg5 gives White some advantage; e.g. 14...h6 15 bxc5! dxc5 (15...hxg5 16 cxd6 g4 17 Ng5 leaves White with a
strong attack and two pawns for the piece; pawns which totally impede Black's
development) 16 Nh3 and White is on top thanks to the e5-pawn and is threatening to start attacking on the queenside, such as with b2-b4 (again!).

9 f5

This plan shouldn't be surprising by now.

9...Na5

As usual 9...gxf5 10 Qh4 gives White very good play for the pawn.

10 fxg6 hxg6 11 Bb3 Nxb3 12 axb3 (Diagram 23)

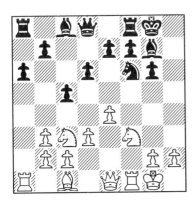 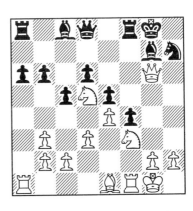

Diagram 23 (B)	Diagram 24 (B)
White plans Qe1-h4 as usual	The bishop joins the attack

12...Nh7

Aiming to impede Qe1-h4, but it doesn't really succeed. However, it's hard to offer good alternatives for Black; for instance, after 12...Bg4 13 Qh4 b5 14 Bh6 Qd7 15
Ng5 Bh5 16 Bxg7 Kxg7 17 h3 Rh8 18 Qf4 the black bishop on h5 is ultimately going
to fall (if White wishes), while Nd5 is also a very strong threat.

13 Qh4 e6 14 Bg5!

Naturally White wants to keep the queens on to continue his attack.

14...f6 15 Bd2

Now White can change his point of attack to the weak g6 and d6-pawns.

15...f5?!

This drops a pawn but Black's position is horrendous already. His best chance is
15...Bd7 16 Qg3 Be8, when White has a range of options; for example, 17 Bf4 (17
Nh4 g5 18 Nf3 followed by h2-h4 also looks strong) 17...e5 18 Be3 f5 19 Bg5 Nxg5

85

20 Nxg5 Qd7 21 Nd5 leaves White with a decisive advantage.

16 Qg3! e5

If 16...Rf6 17 Rae1! b6 18 e5 dxe5 19 Nxe5 Qc7 20 Rf3! Bb7 21 Nxg6 wins.

17 Nd5!

The g6-pawn will fall regardless, so first White takes the central outpost. The immediate 17 Qxg6 would allow 17...Qf6 when Black survives for the moment, albeit a pawn down.

17...f4 18 Qxg6 b6 19 Be1! (Diagram 24)

Bringing the bishop round to h4 so that it can participate in White's attack.

19...Rf7 20 Bh4 Qf8 21 Nxb6

Black drops another pawn.

21...Raa7 22 Nxc8 1-0

Black resigned as he's losing a third pawn after 22...Qxc8 23 Qxd6, and White's attack has still not subsided.

Conclusion

It used to be thought that 8...0-0 9 f5 was too dangerous for Black and so 8...h6 was preferred, but the recent discovery of 9...gxf5 looks to have made this line playable again. I still believe White has adequate compensation after 9 f5!?, but otherwise 9 a3 in Game 14 is a valid alternative, while 5 Bb5+!? and if 5...Bd7 then 6 Bc4 also looks interesting. White has good attacking chances in this 2...d6 line. Black has to play very accurately to survive and we have seen that even the world's top players can lose quickly.

Chapter Four

2...e6 3 f4

The First Few Moves

Illustrative Games

Conclusion

The First Few Moves

1 e4 c5 2 Nc3 e6

2...e6 is the move recommended by Richard Palliser in his book *Fighting the Anti-Sicilians*. That it's not as common as 2...d6 or 2...Nc6 has, I think, to do with the fact that, after 3 Nf3, Black has to be happy playing an Open Sicilian with his pawn already on e6. This cuts down his options significantly as he can no longer play such popular variations as the Najdorf, Sveshnikov or Dragon.

I must admit I find 2...e6 slightly annoying to face as White cannot employ his usual Grand Prix plans and the dynamics of the game are different. Black is able to get the ...d7-d5 break in instantly, so White's kingside attack needs to be prepared with much more detail than normal if it is going to succeed. Instead, White should play against Black's advanced centre and try to prove that it's a weakness.

3 f4 Nc6

This could of course arise from Black playing 2...Nc6 and 3...e6.

3...d5 **(Diagram 1)** straight away is also possible and sometimes transposes:

Diagram 1 (W)
Black plays 3...d5

Diagram 2 (W)
Black plays 4...a6

a) 4 d3 was played by the strong grandmaster Vlastimil Hort and after 4...dxe4 5 dxe4 Qxd1 6 Kxd1 I believe White has a fractional edge, which he successfully converted. However, Black could simply play 4...Nc6, when White can no longer reply with Bf1-b5 and so has, in effect, lost a tempo on the 4...a6 lines below.

b) 4 Nf3 dxe4 (4...Nc6 transposes to our main line) 5 Nxe4 is the so-called 'Toilet Variation' invented by GM Mark Hebden, which is examined (along with 4...Nf6) in Games 21 and 22.

4 Nf3 d5

After 4...a6 **(Diagram 2)** White can no longer develop the bishop to b5, while on c4 it will be hit instantly with ...b7-b5. Therefore, if he still doesn't want to enter a mainline Sicilian with 5 d4 cxd4 6 Nxd4 (specifically a Taimanov with 6 f4), White has either to fianchetto his bishop and play a Closed Sicilian structure (i.e. 5 g3 d5 6 d3 Nf6 7 Bg2) or develop his bishop on e2 (which looks slightly passive). These two options are covered in Games 18 and 19.

A third option, 4...d6, can arise in numerous different ways as Black can play ...d7-d6, ...e7-e6, and ...Nc6 in pretty much any order. Then 5 d4 cxd4 6 Nxd4 Nf6 is a Scheveningen, and otherwise White generally develops the f1-bishop to b5 or c4, or goes for the Closed structure with g2-g3 and d2-d3. Instead, I tried 5 g4! recently, for which see Game 20.

5 Bb5 (Diagram 3)

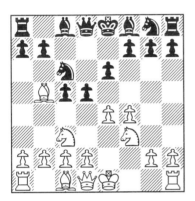

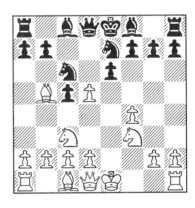

Diagram 3 (B)	Diagram 4 (B)
White threatens 6 Bxc6	Position after 6 exd5

White's aim is to capture on c6 and reach positions similar to those in Chapter Six. If Black is forced to recapture with the b-pawn, his structure is damaged and his queenside counterplay reduced, there being no ...b7-b5-b4 break.

5...Nge7

Intending to follow with 6...a6, when after 7 Bxc6 Nxc6 Black will have the two bishops and no weaknesses in his structure.

a) 5...Nf6 6 Bxc6+ bxc6 7 Qe2 Be7 8 d3 0-0 9 0-0 Qc7 10 Na4 a5 11 c4 Re8 12 b3 Nd7 13 e5 f6 14 Ba3 gave White a very favourable position in G.Kasparov-D.Garrido Fernandez, Cordoba (simul) 1992.

b) 5...d4 is too committal: Black forces the c3-knight to retreat but he also closes the centre and weakens the e5 and c4-squares. After 6 Ne2 (6 Bxc6+ bxc6 7 Ne2 d3! is less clear) 6...Bd7 (6...Nf6 7 Bxc6+ bxc6 8 d3 is good for White) 7 0-0 Nf6 8 d3 Be7

9 Bxc6 Bxc6 10 Ne5 White was slightly better in H.Hamdouchi-L.Marin, Sitges 1995, which continued 10...Rc8 11 g4!? (very ambitious, expanding on the kingside – note that White could not play this way if Black had a break in the centre, but thanks to the early ...d5-d4 White's king should be safe) 11...Nd7 12 Nxc6 Rxc6 13 Ng3 Bh4 14 g5 h6 15 Qh5 Bxg3 16 hxg3 g6 17 Qh3 h5 18 b3 f6 19 f5 exf5 20 exf5 Kf7 21 gxf6 Nxf6 22 Bg5 Qd5 23 Rae1 Re8 24 Rxe8 Nxe8 25 g4 Ng7 26 Qh4 hxg4? 27 fxg6+ and Black resigned.

6 exd5 (Diagram 4)

The main move for White, after which Black has two options: 6...exd5 7 Qe2, threatening to take on c6 doubling Black's pawns; and 6...Nxd5!?, when Black hopes his strong knight will compensate for his bad pawn structure. These are examined in the first game below.

Others:

a) 6 0-0 a6 7 Bxc6+ Nxc6 is very comfortable for Black.

b) 6 Ne5!? was tried in N.Short-V.Topalov, Dos Hermanas 1997, but Black got a good position after 6...Bd7 7 Nxd7 Qxd7 8 exd5?! exd5 9 0-0 0-0-0!. White might play differently, but I cannot find any lines which are troubling for Black.

c) 6 Qe2!? threatens to take on c6 without having to give up his centre, and 6...dxe4 7 Ne5! looks good for White; e.g. 7...Bd7 8 Nxe4 (threatening mate!) 8...Nd5 9 Bxc6 Bxc6 10 Nxc6 bxc6 11 d3 Be7 12 0-0 with the advantage. However, this seems a better moment for 6...d4!, and 7 Nd1 a6 8 Bxc6+ Nxc6 9 d3 Be7 10 0-0 b6 11 Nf2 Bb7 was fine for Black in T.L.Petrosian-Art.Minasian, Batumi 2003.

Statistics

White hasn't scored particularly well in this line (47%), winning 888 and losing 1072 out of 2642 games in my database, but in these Black had a significantly higher average rating: 2202, as opposed to 2151 for White. Between top players White has scored 44% recently, but this was also against higher rated opposition, so it's about as expected. I think a reason for the comparatively low score is that White has to adjust his plans somewhat in this line, but objectively I believe he still has good chances for an advantage.

Illustrative Games

Game 17
☐ **S.Iuldachev** ◼ **A.El Arousy**
Abu Dhabi 2003

1 e4 c5 2 Nc3 Nc6 3 f4 e6 4 Nf3 d5 5 Bb5 Nge7 6 exd5 exd5

...Nxd5!? **(Diagram 5)** is the move recommended by Palliser, when White has three main options:

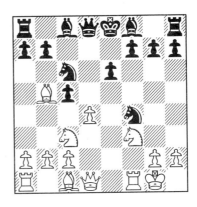

Diagram 5 (W)

Black plays 6...Nxd5!?

Diagram 6 (B)

Position after 8 d4

a) 7 Bxc6+ is the one White would like to play, but Black has a few tricks to retain equality: 7...bxc6 8 Ne5 (8 d3 c4!) 8...Bd6! 9 d3 (9 0-0 Nxf4! is Black's idea) 9...Bxe5 10 fxe5 Qh4+ 11 g3 Qd4, as in Art.Minasian-J.Becerra Rivero, World Team Championship, Lucerne 1997, when Black's activity makes up for his bad pawn structure.

b) 7 Ne5 is the main move, and was employed by former World Champion Smyslov back in 1959. 7...Bd7 8 Bxc6 Bxc6 9 Nxc6 bxc6 10 0-0 Be7 has been reached numerous times when White has the superior pawn structure, but Black has that strong knight on d5 so chances are probably about balanced. (Notably Black was never troubled in V.Smyslov-F.Olafsson, Bled/Zagreb/Belgrade Candidates 1959.)

c) 7 0-0 seems most in the spirit of the Grand Prix, and then:

c1) 7...Be7 8 Bxc6+ bxc6 9 Ne5 is a good version of the 7 Bxc6+ line for White, as the black bishop is less actively placed on e7. Then 9...Qc7 10 d3 0-0 11 Ne4 f6 12 Nc4 f5 13 Ng3 Bf6 14 Qe2 Nb6 15 Ne5 gave White a very comfortable game in Art.Minasian-B.Alterman, Manila Olympiad 1992.

c2) 7...Bd7 allows 8 Nxd5!? exd5 9 Re1+ Be7 10 Bxc6 Bxc6 (if 10...bxc6 11 Ne5 or 11 Qe2!?) 11 Qe2 with an edge as Black has difficulties castling.

c3) 7...Nxf4 is critical, although it's been played surprisingly rarely – only four times in my database. For the pawn White gets typical Grand Prix Attack compensation: the semi-open f-file to attack down, a lead in development and the better structure (after he captures on c6). 8 d4 **(Diagram 6)** looks to be the best response, but it needs some testing in games.

c31) 8...cxd4 9 Ne5 (neither 9 Qxd4 Qxd4+ 10 Nxd4 Bc5! 11 Rxf4 e5, nor 9 Bxf4 dxc3 10 Qxd8+ Kxd8 11 Rad1+ Ke8 12 bxc3, offers White anything, while 12 Ne5 Bc5+ 13 Kh1 a6 14 Ba4 cxb2 15 Nxc6 Bd7 looks good for Black) 9...dxc3 10 Qxd8+ Kxd8 11 Nxf7+ Kc7 is a messy line given by Palliser, in which Black has compensation for the exchange, but I think White holds the edge after 12 Nxh8 (12 Bxf4+ e5 13 Be3 cxb2 14 Rab1 Rg8 is unclear) 12...e5 13 Nf7 or 12...Bc5+ 13 Kh1 e5 14 Nf7.

c32) 8...Ng6 9 Be3 (also possible is 9 d5!? exd5 10 Nxd5 Be6 11 c4 with compensation, while 10 Ng5!? Be6 11 Qh5 Be7 12 Nxe6 fxe6 13 Bd3 Nce5 14 Bb5+ Nc6 repeats for a draw) 9...cxd4 10 Nxd4 Bd7 11 Qf3 (11 Nxc6 Bxc6 12 Bxc6+ bxc6 13 Qf3 looks reasonable as well) 11...Qf6 12 Qxf6 (Palliser's 12 Qe2 Qe5 13 Qf2 f6 is unclear, though White has good compensation here too) 12...gxf6 13 Ne4! Nxd4 14 Bxd7+ Kxd7 15 Rad1!? e5 16 c3 f5 17 Rxf5 Ke6 18 Rf6+ Kd5 19 Ng3 **(Diagram 7)** and White seems slightly better.

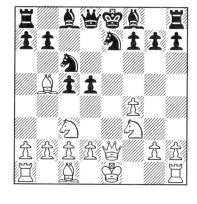

Diagram 7 (B)	Diagram 8 (B)
White seems slightly better	Position after 7 Qe2

We'll have to await more practical tests, but I'm confident White has at least enough compensation in this line.

7 Qe2 (Diagram 8) 7...Qd6

Instead:

a) 7...Be6 does not deter 8 Bxc6+ as 8...Nxc6?? 9 f5 drops a piece.

b) 7...Bg4!? (Black goes for counterplay rather than bothering about damage to his pawn structure) 8 Bxc6+ bxc6 9 0-0 Qd6 (if 9...g6!? then 10 Qe5 Rg8 11 d3 Bg7 12 Qe1 gives White the edge) and now 10 b3! looks stronger than the normal 10 h3. White's plan is Bc1-a3 to target the weak c5-pawn.

b1) 10...Qxf4 (10...Qe6 11 Qf2) 11 Ba3 and Black's c5-pawn is in trouble: 11...Bxf3 12 Rxf3 Qd4+ 13 Kh1 and although Black has managed to win a pawn, he has no vay to develop his pieces and cannot prevent White's simple plan of Raf1 hitting 7; e.g. 13...Rd8 14 Raf1 f6 15 Na4 with a decisive advantage.

)2) If Black tries to develop with 10...g6, White can grab the long diagonal with 11 3b2 Bg7 12 Nb5! cxb5 13 Bxg7 Rg8 14 Bb2 and White is clearly better.

)3) 10...0-0-0?! is no improvement: 11 Qa6+ Kb8 12 Ne5 Be6 13 Ba3 f6 14 Nd3 Nf5 15 Bxc5 Qc7 16 Bxf8 Bc8 17 Nb4! Rdxf8 18 Nxc6+ Ka8 19 Nxd5 1-0 B.Heberla-K.Singer, Polish Junior Championships, Bartkowa 2002.

:) 7...g6!? was employed by Michael Stean back in the 1970s and is enjoying a cur-'ent revival with GMs Shirov and Nataf trying it as Black. The point is that after 8 Qe5 Black can gain time on White's queen to complete his development, even if it s a slightly unorthodox type of development: 8...Rg8 9 0-0 Bg7 10 Qe1!? Kf8 is :ather unclear. I faced this line myself against Nataf and I tried 8 Ne5 Be6 9 b3 Rc8 10 Bb2 Rg8! 11 0-0-0 a6, G.Jones-I.Nataf, European Championship, Dresden 2007, reaching a very messy position which eventually ended in a draw. It seems in-credible that Black can get away with moves such as ...Rg8 but his position seems solid enough to hold, if you're over 2600 anyway!

For White, 8 Qe3!? hitting the c5-pawn looks like a good try, the point being that after 8...Qd6 (8...d4? runs into 9 Qe5!) 9 d4! cxd4 10 Qxd4 is good for White.

8 d4! (Diagram 9)

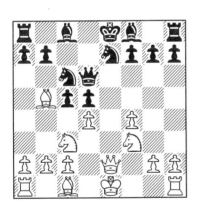

Diagram 9 (B)	Diagram 10 (B)
White breaks in the centre	The b5-bishop is untouchable

Breaking in the centre seems strong since it will still take Black a few moves to complete his development. 8 0-0, 8 Ne5 and 8 Bxc6+ have also been tried but do not seem as convincing as the text.

8...cxd4

8...c4 9 0-0 (the immediate 9 b3 might be even stronger) 9...f6 10 b3! can result in a quick victory for White. Black's king is in deep trouble stuck in the centre of the board: 10...cxb3 11 axb3 a6 12 Re1 Bd7? 13 Ba3 Nb4 14 Bxd7+ Kxd7 15 Na2 Nec6 1-0 D.Campora-A.Martinez Fernandez, Coria del Rio 2002.

9 Nxd4 Bd7

On 9...a6 Bangiev's suggestion of 10 f5!! **(Diagram 10)** seems very strong. The bishop on b5 cannot be taken: 10...axb5 11 Ndxb5 Qd7 12 Bf4 threatens both Nc7+ and Nd6+ which cannot be parried (12...Kd8 is clearly hopeless), while 10...Rb8 also runs into trouble down the h2-b8 diagonal after 11 0-0! axb5 12 Ndxb5 Qe5 13 Qf2 with Bf4 coming next move. Black's best is probably 10...Bd7, but then 11 Nxc6 bxc6 12 Bd3 offers White a strong initiative, e.g. 12...g6 13 0-0! Bxf5 14 Bf4 Qc5+ 15 Kh1 or 13...Bg7 14 Bf4 Qc5+ 15 Be3 Qd6 16 Na4.

9...g6 10 Be3 Bg7 11 0-0 0-0 12 Qf2 is also favourable for White with his superior pawn structure. He can play against the isolated d5-pawn or take on c6 to give Black hanging pawns. After 12...Qb4 13 Bxc6 bxc6 14 Nb3 Qb7 15 Rfe1 Re8 16 Bd4 Bxd4 17 Qxd4 White's control of the important d4 and c5-squares gave him the edge in M.Rudolf-B.Sygulski, Polish Team Championship 2004, which concluded swiftly 17...Qb6 18 Nc5! Qxb2? 19 Rab1 Qxc2 20 Re2 Qf5 21 Rbe1 Be6 22 Nxe6 fxe6 23 Rxe6 Qf7 24 Qe5 1-0.

10 Bxc6!

Gaining time in order to complete his development. White has a simple plan: he will drop his knight back to b3 and play Be3 to control the c5 and d4-squares, after which he will have a clear advantage.

10...bxc6 11 0-0 g6 12 Nb3! Bg7 13 Be3 Be6

13...d4 14 Rad1 c5 fails to 15 Ne4 and 16 Nxc5.

14 Bc5 Qd7 15 Bd4! (Diagram 11)

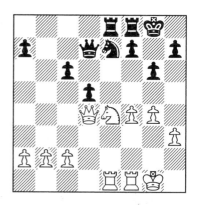

Diagram 11 (B)	Diagram 12 (B)
Trading dark-squared bishops	The knight heads for f6

A clever move, forcing the trade of dark-squared bishops and leaving Black's king slightly exposed. Black will now have no way of challenging White's dark square control.

15...Bg4

15...Bxd4+ 16 Nxd4 0-0 17 Na4! Qd6 18 Qe5 Rfd8 19 Qxd6 Rxd6 20 Nc5 gives White a pleasant edge, as his knights cannot be dislodged.

16 Qf2 Bxd4 17 Qxd4 0-0 18 Nc5

White's strategy has been successful and he holds all the trumps of the position.

18...Qc7 19 h3 Bf5

In view of White's next move, 19...Bc8 might be better, when 20 g4 could be answered by 20...h5.

20 g4!

White does not want his queen to be dislodged from its powerful square in the centre of the board and so goes to an extreme to prevent ...Nf5. This may look as though it weakens his king, but Black has no way to exploit it with his pieces so passive.

20...Bd7?!

20...Bxc2 is probably Black's best try, but White retains the advantage after 21 Rac1 Be4 22 N3xe4 dxe4 23 Nxe4.

21 Rae1

21 N3e4 dxe4 22 Nxd7 Rad8 23 Rad1 was another option.

21...Rae8 22 Nxd7 Qxd7 23 Ne4! (Diagram 12)

White uses the pin to bring his knight to the strong f6-square.

23...f6?

23...f5 was necessary, but White is still winning the exchange after 24 Nf6+ Rxf6 25 Qxf6 fxg4 26 Re6, while 24 Nc5!? Qd6 25 Re6 also came into consideration.

24 Nxf6+ Rxf6 25 Qxf6 Nc8 26 f5 1-0

Game 18
☐ **O.Ekebjaerg** ■ **S.Lundholm**
Correspondence 1989

---

1 Nc3!? c5 2 f4 Nc6 3 e4

A bizarre move order to reach the Grand Prix Attack!

3...e6 4 Nf3 a6 (Diagram 13)

Black plays another typical Sicilian move, still allowing White to return to the main lines with d2-d4 if he so wishes. 4...a6 also rules out the option of Bf1-b5, so

White decides to fianchetto his bishop instead. The alternative development, 5 Be2, is considered in the next game.

5 g3 d5

5...d6 6 Bg2 g6 7 d4! cxd4 8 Nxd4 gives White a good version of a mainline Sicilian, as ...e7-e6 and ...g7-g6 don't really work well together; e.g. 8...Nge7 9 Be3 Bg7 10 Qd2 0-0 11 0-0-0 with a clear advantage in D.Campora-M.Garcia Carbo, Candas 1992.

6 d3

White wants to keep some tension in the centre. Instead 6 e5, the move suggested in *Chess Openings for White, Explained*, feels dubious as it gifts Black the f5-square. Then 6...Nge7 7 Bh3!? b5 8 0-0 Qb6 9 Kh1 g6, as given by Rogozenko, looks good for Black, since White doesn't appear to have a constructive plan.

6...d4?! (Diagram 14)

Diagram 13 (W)

Black plays 4...a6

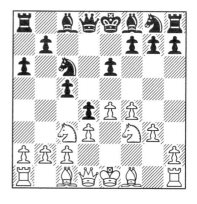

Diagram 14 (W)

A premature advance

A tempting but flawed move. Black gains a tempo on the white knight but closes the centre prematurely, allowing White to concentrate on his kingside assault. Furthermore, in these lines White normally wants to manoeuvre his c3-knight elsewhere anyway.

Instead:

a) 6...dxe4 7 Nxe4 Nh6 (7...Nf6 8 Bg2 Nxe4 9 dxe4 Qxd1+ 10 Kxd1 b5 11 c3 Bb7 12 Be3 Be7 13 Nd2 Na5 14 Kc2 gave White an edge in G.Jones-C.Pritchett, British League 2005, due to his space on the kingside and better central control; the king is actually better placed on c2 as it's ready for the endgame) 8 Bg2 Nf5 9 0-0 Be7 10 c3 and White was slightly better in A.Cabrera-M.Illescas Cordoba, Albox 2005, when Black blundered with 10...b6? 11 g4! Nd6 12 Ne5 Nxe5 13 Nxd6+ Qxd6 14 fxe5 Qb8 15 Qf3! and wins.

b) 6...Nge7 7 Bg2 g6 8 0-0 Bg7 9 a3!? (9 Qe2 0-0 10 Kh1 d4 11 Nd1 f5 12 c3 h6 13 Bd2 was unclear in V.Zhelnin-V.Vasiliev, Tula 2000) 9...b5 10 Bd2 Bb7 11 Rb1 0-0 12 b4 Qb6 13 Kh1 d4 14 Ne2 h6 15 Be1 Rfd8 16 Bf2 cxb4 17 axb4 Qc7 18 Nc1 Nc8 19 Nb3 Nxb4 20 Nbxd4 was somewhat better for White in W.Arencibia-L.Van Wely, Yerevan Olympiad 1996.

c) 6...Nf6 **(Diagram 15)** is critical and has been played by such top grandmasters as Ivanchuk and Judit Polgar.

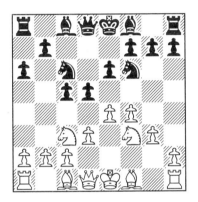
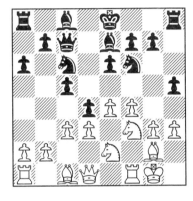

| **Diagram 15 (W)** | **Diagram 16 (B)** |
| The critical 6...Nf6 | Breaking open the centre |

c1) 7 e5 (better than on the previous move, as White now gains a tempo on the black knight and it can no longer jump into f5) 7...Nd7 (7...d4!? is also possible) 8 Bg2 b5 9 0-0 Be7 10 Qe1 b4 11 Nd1 0-0, was S.Lalic-T.Luther, Hastings 1994/95, and now T.Horvath's 12 Ne3 a5 13 h4 would offer White good attacking chances.

c2) 7 Bg2 Be7 8 0-0 0-0 9 Ne5 (another option is 9 Qe2 b5 10 Nd1, rerouting the knight to f2 so that White can possibly play the g4-g5 break, while the knight won't be attacked on c3 if Black plays ...Nd4 and White wants to recapture; e.g. 10...dxe4 11 dxe4 Nd4 12 Nxd4 cxd4 13 Nf2 Bb7 14 b3 Rc8 15 Bb2 Qc7 16 Rac1 Rfd8 17 Nd3 was unclear in J.Hickl-J.Ehlvest, Zagreb Interzonal 1987) 9...Nd4 (9...Nxe5?! 10 fxe5 is very pleasant for White, e.g. 10...Nd7 11 exd5 Nxe5 12 Qh5 Ng6 13 Be3 with a clear advantage, S.Dumont-V.Marques, Sao Paulo 1999) 10 exd5 (10 g4!? is very aggressive, but the pawn storms generally don't work as well when the centre is still fluid; e.g. 10...dxe4 11 dxe4 b5 12 g5 Nd7 13 Nf3 Bb7 14 Kh1 b4 15 Nxd4 cxd4 16 Ne2 Nc5 and Black was doing well in L.Aronian-V.Ivanchuk, Monte Carlo (rapid) 2006; 11 Nxe4 may be a slight improvement) 10...Nxd5 (10...exd5 11 g4 now leads to interesting play) 11 Nxd5 exd5 12 Be3 f6 13 Nf3 Nc6 14 d4! and White was perhaps a little better in N.Short-J.Polgar, Buenos Aires 2001.

7 Ne2 Nf6 8 Bg2 Be7 9 0-0 Qc7 10 h3

Preparing to push on the kingside with g3-g4.

10...h5?!

A natural retort, but Black lives to regret this weakening: his king now has no safe square to go to, whereas White can easily switch plans.

11 c3! (Diagram 16)

Breaking open the centre while Black's king is stuck there.

11...Bd7

11...dxc3 12 bxc3 leaves White in complete control of the centre and with the possibility of play down the semi-open b-file.

12 cxd4 cxd4 13 b3!

Preparing to gang up on the d4-pawn with Bb2. Taking straight away wasn't possible due to 13 Nexd4 Nxd4 14 Nxd4 Bc5 15 Be3 Qb6.

13...Rd8 14 Bb2 Qb8

Black is playing without any real plan. He feels his king would be even weaker on g8, but probably he should try castling anyway, just so he can complete his development. As the game progresses Black goes down without any counterplay.

15 Rc1 (Diagram 17)

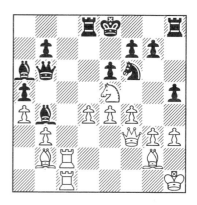

Diagram 17 (B)	Diagram 18 (B)
The d4-pawn is doomed	White holds all the trumps

White simply completes his development, while Black still cannot find a safe square for his king. The pawn on d4 is doomed, so White should have a technically winning position.

15...Nb4 16 a3 Na2

Trying to complicate the issue.

17 Rc2 Nc3 18 Nxc3 dxc3 19 Rxc3 Qa7+ 20 Kh1 Bb5 21 Ne5

The white knight jumps into the centre of the board, while answering the threat of ...Nxe4.

21...a5 22 a4 Ba6 23 Qf3 Qb6 24 Rfc1

Threatening to penetrate on the back rank.

24...Bd6 25 d4!

The pawn is invulnerable as 25...Qxd4? allows 26 Nxf7! Kxf7 27 Rc7+.

25...Bb4 26 R3c2 (Diagram 18)

White holds all the trumps in this position. He has a strong central pawn mass, a monster knight on e5, a safe king, rooks doubled on the c-file – and furthermore is a pawn up!

26...Rh6 27 Qe3 Nd7 28 Nc4 Qa7 29 Bc3 e5

Black tries desperately to unbalance the position but White has it all under control.

30 fxe5 Bxc4 31 bxc4 Nxe5 32 Qg5 Nd3 33 Rf1

Moving in for the kill.

33...Rg6

If 33...Bxc3 34 Qxg7 wins.

34 Qb5+ Ke7 35 Rf3 Bxc3 36 Rxc3 Ne1 37 Qe5+ 1-0

If 37...Re6 38 Qc7+ Rd7 39 Rxf7+ wins, while after 37...Kf8 38 Qc7 hits the rook and threatens mate on f7. A complete rout.

Game 19
☐ **J.E. Lutton** ■ **M.Dougherty**
Isle of Man 2002

---

1 Nc3!? c5 2 e4 e6 3 f4 a6 4 Nf3 Nc6 5 Be2!? (Diagram 19)

An interesting alternative to fianchettoing the bishop, so White can play with the typical Grand Prix plan of Qe1-h4, etc.

5...d5 6 d3 Nf6

Instead:

a) 6...g6 7 0-0 Bg7 8 Qe1 Nge7 9 Kh1 b5 10 Qf2 d4 11 Nb1! 0-0 12 Nbd2 e5 13 fxe5 Nxe5 14 Nxe5 Bxe5 offers White good play, M.Hebden-J.Plaskett, Charlton 1983.

b) 6...dxe4 7 dxe4 Qc7 (7...Qxd1+ 8 Bxd1 leaves White with an edge) 8 0-0 b5 9 e5 Nge7? (9...Bb7) 10 Bxb5! won a pawn in E.Pessi-L.Vajda, Miercurea Ciuc 1998, since 10...axb5? loses to 11 Nxb5 and 12 Nd6+.

7 0-0 Be7 8 Qe1 d4

As in the previous game, the advance ...d5-d4 is rather committal, as it allows White to attack on the kingside without having to worry about the centre being opened up. 8...0-0 looks more sensible, when after 9 Qg3 chances are about balanced.

9 Nb1! (Diagram 20)

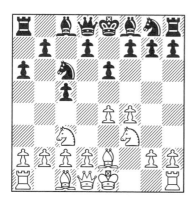
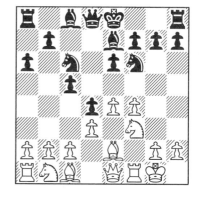

Diagram 19 (B)	Diagram 20 (B)
White plays 5 Be2!?	The knight will reappear on d2

 NOTE: It looks odd to retreat the knight back to its starting square, but Black has weakened himself by advancing the d-pawn, so White can afford a couple of tempi to bring that knight round to d2 and then either to c4 or e4 (after pushing e4-e5).

9...b5 10 Ne5!

Taking the inviting central square. Black does not want to exchange on e5, as this would leave White with lots of play down the f- and g-files, as well as allowing the c1-bishop access all the way down the c1-h6 diagonal. Black must therefore defend his knight.

10...Bb7 11 Qg3 0-0 12 Nxc6

Not 12 f5??, as 12...Nxe5 13 Qxe5 Bd6 embarrasses the white queen.

12...Bxc6 13 f5

White has obtained typical kingside play.

13...Kh8 14 Nd2

The knight re-enters the game, but perhaps 14 fxe6 fxe6 15 Bf4 is slightly more accurate, ruling out Black's possibility on his next move, so White can hope for a small edge.

14...e5 (Diagram 21)

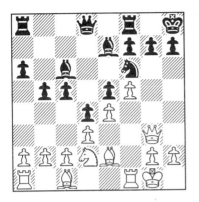

Diagram 21 (W)	**Diagram 22 (B)**
Black has no counterplay	A pretty knight sacrifice

Black, understandably, did not want to allow f5xe6, but now the centre has been closed off completely, meaning that White's attack can gather momentum. Instead, Black should take the time for 14...Qb8 when the chances remain balanced. The exchange of queens would limit the white attack, while after 15 Qh3 (15 e5 Nd7) 15...exf5, the desirable 16 Rxf5 now runs into 16...Bd7.

15 Nf3

15 Qxe5?? Bd6 was Black's trick.

15...Nd7 16 Bg5 f6

16...Bxg5 17 Nxg5 Qf6 might be a better defensive try.

17 Bd2 c4 18 Nh4!

Exploiting the weakening of g6.

18...Qe8 19 Ng6+!! (Diagram 22)

A thematic, but very pretty knight sacrifice. Black has no defence against the plan of mate on h7 as his pieces all get in the way of each other.

19...hxg6 20 fxg6 Kg8 21 Rf5 Nc5 22 Rh5 1-0

There is no defence to the threat of 23 Rh8+ Kxh8 24 Qh4+ Kg8 25 Qh7 mate.

Game 20
☐ **G.Jones** ■ **K.Arakhamia**
British League 2006

---

1 e4 c5 2 Nc3 e6 3 f4 Nc6 4 Nf3 d6

This position could be reached via any of the main second moves for Black; e.g. 2...Nc6 3 f4 d6 4 Nf3 e6, or 2...d6 3 f4 e6 4 Nf3 Nc6.

5 g4! (Diagram 23)

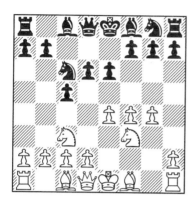

Diagram 23 (B)	Diagram 24 (B)
An aggressive lunge	Queens are not required

I discovered this move over the board. Presuming that White doesn't want to open the Sicilian with d2-d4, the usual move has been 5 Bb5, but after 5...Nge7 6 0-0 a6 7 Bxc6+ (7 Be2 b5 is hardly inspiring) 7...Nxc6 we have a position similar to the 3 Bb5 lines seen later in this book, except that here Black has no structural weaknesses.

Although 5 g4 is a strange-looking move, it has its points. In the 4...a6 variation, one of White's options is to set up in Closed Sicilian fashion with 5 g3 (as in Game 18). However, 5 g3 here would in effect lose a tempo, as Black is not forced to play ...a7-a6. The danger with g2-g4 is that White might find himself exposed if Black can open the position quickly, but that would involve playing ...d6-d5, having already spent a move on ...d7-d6.

5...Nge7

The position is already tricky for Black. If 5...Nf6 then 6 g5 is awkward, while 5...h5 doesn't achieve anything after 6 g5. Instead, 5...g6 6 Bg2 gives White a favourable type of Closed Sicilian, since he has managed to play g2-g4 without first inserting g2-g3, while Black has delayed breaking with ...d5. White's plan will be to castle kingside, play d2-d3, reroute his knight from c3 to g3, and break with f4-f5. Alternatively, 6 h4!? looks very interesting, too. White is happy to castle queenside if necessary, while Black has no satisfactory squares for her king.

6 d3 d5

A sign that things have not gone to plan for Black. 6...g6 can be dealt with as before by either 7 Bg2 or 7 h4!?.

7 Bg2 dxe4?!

Black swaps off queens mistakenly thinking this will blunt the attack. Instead, she should play 7...g6 and try to weather the storm, although White's position is definitely preferable.

8 dxe4 Qxd1+ 9 Kxd1!

White does not worry about the slight inconvenience to his king. Now Nc3-b5 is threatened, after which it is hard to prevent Nc7+, so Black is forced to create another hole in her position.

9...a6

If 9...Bd7 10 Nb5 0-0-0 11 Nd6+ or 10...Kd8 11 Nd6 wins, while 9...Ng6 10 Nb5 Kd7 11 Ke2 and if 11...a6 12 Rd1+ is clearly better for White. *Fritz* goes as far as to suggest 9...Ng8, which just shows the lack of coordination between Black's pieces.

10 Na4 Ng6 11 f5 (Diagram 24) 11...Nge5 12 Nxe5 Nxe5 13 Nb6 Rb8 14 Bf4 Bd6 15 Ke2 0-0

Perhaps it was better to keep the king in the centre of the board with 15...Ke7, but White still has a big advantage with his pieces developing swiftly and a strong knight on b6.

16 Rad1 Bc7 17 Nc4 f6

17...Nxc4 18 Bxc7 Ra8 19 b3 Na3 20 Bd6 is hopeless for Black.

18 Bxe5 fxe5

If 18...Bxe5 19 Nxe5 fxe5 20 Rd6 Kf7 21 Rhd1 completely clamps down on Black, who will find it very difficult to move any of her pieces.

19 Rd2 b5 20 Nd6 c4 21 Rhd1 (Diagram 25)

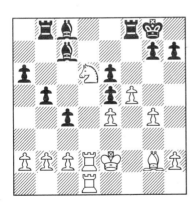

Diagram 25 (B)

White controls the board

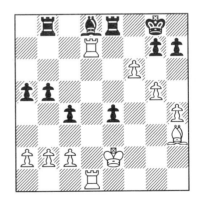

Diagram 26 (B)

Opening up the king

White has a lovely position here, as the knight on d6 and doubled rooks on the d-file control the board. Black would like to get rid of her doubled e-pawns with 21...exf5, but that would allow White's final piece, the light-squared bishop, to enter the game on the long diagonal after 22 exf5.

21...a5 22 Nxc8 Rbxc8 23 Rd7

Stopping Black from swapping rooks to relieve the pressure with 23...Rfd8, as that now allows 24 Rxc7. There is no need to take the e6-pawn yet and give Black the open f-file.

23...Rfe8 24 g5 Bd8 25 h4 exf5 26 exf5 e4

Desperately trying to keep White's final piece out of the game, but it is too late.

27 Bh3

27 Rb7 also gives White a decisive advantage, as 27...Re7 is met by 28 Rxd8+!.

27...Rb8 28 f6! (Diagram 26)

Opening up the black king.

28...gxf6 29 Bf5 fxg5

29...h6 30 gxh6 is equally catastrophic for Black.

30 Bxh7+ Kh8 31 Bg6 Rf8 32 hxg5 Bxg5 33 Rh1+ Kg8 34 Bh7+ Kh8 35 Bxe4+ 1-0

35...Kg8 36 Bd5+ wins everything.

Game 21
☐ **S.Tiviakov** ◼ **I.Kurnosov**
European Championship, Istanbul 2003

---

1 e4 c5 2 Nc3 e6 3 f4 d5

Instead of rejoining the main lines with 3...Nc6, Black utilizes his 2...e6 move order to break in the centre straight away.

4 Nf3 dxe4

4...Nc6 is still possible and returns to Game 17 above. Another option is 4...Nf6 5 Bb5+ (Minasian has preferred to play in quiet style with 5 d3 Nc6 6 Be2 Be7 7 0-0 reaching a similar type of position to that in Game 19; Art.Minasian-F.Akintola, Turin Olympiad 2006, continued 7...b6 8 Qe1 Bb7 9 e5 Nd7 10 f5! exf5 11 Qg3 and White was clearly better), and now **(Diagram 27)**:

a) 5...Nc6 6 d3 Be7 7 Bxc6+ bxc6 8 0-0 Ba6 9 e5 Nd7 10 b3 c4 11 dxc4 dxc4 12 Re1 Nb6 13 Ne4 0-0 14 Be3 Nd5 15 Qd2 Nxe3 16 Qxe3 Qb6 17 Rad1 Rfd8 18 Nd6! cxb3 19 axb3 h6 20 Rd1 c5 21 Red1 saw White on top in M.Adams-J.Lautier, Chalkidiki 1992.

b) 5...Bd7 6 Bxd7+ Nbxd7 looks preferable; for example 7 d3 Nb8!? (heading back towards its best square on c6) 8 0-0 (8 Ne5!? dxe4 9 dxe4 Qxd1+ 10 Kxd1 Nbd7 11

Nc4 might offer White a slight advantage) 8...Nc6 9 Bd2 (9 Ne5!? is possible here too) 9...Be7 10 Kh1 0-0 11 Qe1 Nd4! 12 Rc1 Rc8 13 Ne5 b5 14 Nd1! b4 15 c3! bxc3 16 bxc3 Nc6 17 Nxc6! Rxc6 18 e5 Nd7 19 c4! and White was slightly better in S.Sale-J.Ehlvest, Dubai 2001.

5 Nxe4 (Diagram 28)

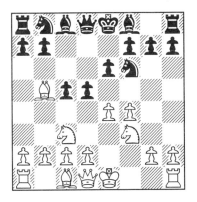

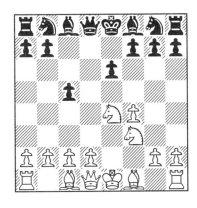

Diagram 27 (B)	Diagram 28 (B)
Black plays 4...Nf6	The 'Toilet Variation'

Transposing to a line of the so-called 'Toilet Variation' (2 f4 d5 3 Nc3), invented by Mark Hebden. Instead, 5 Bb5+ simplifies the position and does not give White much advantage, though 5...Bd7 (5...Nd7!? is an attempt by Black to play for the win) 6 Bxd7+ Nxd7 (6...Qxd7!?) 7 Nxe4 Ngf6 is perhaps a slight nibble.

5...Nd7

Avoiding the typical positions reached after 5...Nc6, which are examined in the next game. Black has also tried:

a) 5...Be7 6 d4! cxd4 (if 6...Nf6 7 Nxc5!) 7 Qxd4 (White happily swaps queens knowing he'll have an edge with his lead in development) 7...Qxd4 8 Nxd4 (threatening 9 Nb5) 8...a6 was M.Adams-J.Lautier, Tilburg 1997, and now Adams suggests 9 g3! Nf6 10 Bg2 Nbd7 11 Bd2! which gives White a nice edge. Black will have problems developing his queenside as the bishop is needed on c8 to defend the b7-pawn. White, on the other hand, is ready to castle queenside and will then have all his pieces ready to start attacking Black's weaknesses, such as the d6-square and the b7-pawn.

b) 5...Nf6 6 Nxf6+ (6 Nf2!?) 6...gxf6 (Black is willing to double his pawns in order to control the crucial e5-square; instead 6...Qxf6 7 g3 Nc6 8 Bg2 h6 9 d3 Bd6 10 0-0 0-0 11 Nd2! Bd7 12 c3 Qd8 13 Nc4 Be7 14 Qe2 was good for White in M.Turov-D.Pudovkin, Krasnodar 2005) 7 b3 Nc6 8 Bb2 Bd7 (J.Houska-S.B.Hansen, German

League 2003), and now the double fianchetto with 9 g3 should give White some advantage.

c) 5...Nh6!? is interesting, with the idea of controlling the d4-square after the knight relocates to f5. In fact I only have two examples of this move. After 6 d4 cxd4 7 Qxd4 Qc7 (Palliser's 7...Qxd4 looks more sensible, but White can claim some advantage in the queenless middlegame with a slight lead in development and the knight now out of place on h6) 8 Bd2 Nc6 9 Qc3 Nf5, rather than 10 0-0-0 Bb4 11 Qd3 0-0 as in W.Watson-B.Kurajica, Amsterdam 1985, Palliser suggests simply 10 a3! with an edge for White.

6 g3 Ngf6

6...Be7 7 Bg2 Ngf6 8 Nf2 Rb8 9 b3 Qc7 10 Bb2 b6 11 Qe2 Bb7 12 0-0 0-0 13 c4! a6 14 Rae1 gave White the upper hand in E.Sveshnikov-I.Jelen, Ljubljana 2002.

7 Nxf6+ Nxf6 8 Bg2 Be7 9 b3

 NOTE: This plan of a double fianchetto is typical of this variation. White's bishops work well together to attack the central squares.

9...0-0 10 Bb2 (Diagram 29)

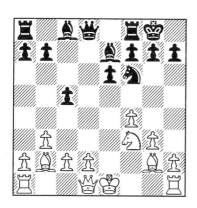 

Diagram 29 (B)	Diagram 30 (B)
A typical double fianchetto	White begins his attack

10...Bd7 11 Ne5

Cutting out Black's ideas of ...Bc6.

11...Qc7 12 Qf3!

Further keeping Black on the defensive.

12...Rab8 13 0-0

White can be very happy with his opening: his bishops rake across the board, he has a strong knight on e5 and has completed his development, whereas Black is very passive. Now White can see about starting an attack on the black king.

13...Bb5?!

Trying for queenside counterplay with 13...b5!? looks like a better plan, though I still prefer White.

14 c4!

Although this leaves the d2-pawn backward, more importantly it controls the d5-square and forces Black's bishop to retreat.

14...Ba6 15 f5! (Diagram 30)

With the black bishop on the offside a6-square White can start his kingside play.

15...exf5 16 Qxf5 Rbd8

Black's only counterplay relies on the weakness of the d2-pawn, but White can defend this easily.

17 Rf2

Defending the pawn and threatening to treble on the f-file.

17...Rd6 18 g4!

Intending to drive the knight away with g4-g5, after which f7 will drop.

18...h6 19 h4 b6

Black attempts to reactivate the a6-bishop.

20 Raf1

20 g5 hxg5 21 hxg5 Bc8 22 Qc2 also looks good for White.

20...Bc8 21 Qf4 Be6

The bishop is back in the game at last, but now White's pieces are all ready for the final assault on Black's king.

22 g5 hxg5 23 hxg5 Nh7 24 Nf3!

Regrouping; White threatens 25 Be5, winning the exchange.

24...Qd8 25 Qe5!

White plays this part of the game very well; Black is forced to create a weakness.

25...f6 26 Qe4 Re8

If 26...Nxg5 27 Nxg5 fxg5 28 Qg6 wins. Black's best might be 26...fxg5 27 Qg6 Rf6! sacrificing the exchange, though White is obviously clearly better.

27 Bc3!

Very calm! Tiviakov defends his d2-pawn before finishing the attack. Black does not have any useful moves and must just wait.

27...Qd7 28 g6 Nf8 29 Nh4 (Diagram 31)

The pawn on g6 is a thorn in Black's side and he must constantly watch out for

White's Qh5 ideas.

29...Bd8 30 Re2 Re7 31 Qf3

This allows Black some counterplay. 31 Qf4 Bc7 32 Nf5! Bxf5 33 Rxe7 Qxe7 34 Qxf5 was probably better, when White has gained a tempo on the game (compare the position after 35 Qxf5 below) and avoided any trouble with ...Rg3.

31...Rd3 32 Qh5

And here 32 Qf4 might be more accurate, preventing an immediate ...Rg3, e.g. 32...Bc7 33 Qe4 Qd6 34 Bf3.

32...Bc7

32...Rg3!? might be more disruptive, intending ...Rg5 to expel the white queen and then remove the annoying g6-pawn.

33 Nf5

Forcing Black to weaken his light squares even more. Alternatively, 33 Rxe6!? Qxe6 34 Nf5 gives White good compensation for the exchange.

33...Bxf5 34 Rxe7 Qxe7 35 Qxf5 Rg3?

It's too late for this now. Instead, if 35...Qd6? 36 Be5! Qxe5 37 Qxd3 wins the exchange, but the computer defence 35...Qe2! seems to hold for Black; e.g. 36 Bxf6 Rxd2 37 Bd5+ Rxd5 38 Qxd5+ (the winning try 38 Be5 Qe3+ 39 Rf2 gets hit by 39...Qg3+!!) 38...Ne6 39 Qa8+ Nf8 40 Qd5+ with a draw.

36 Kf2! (Diagram 32)

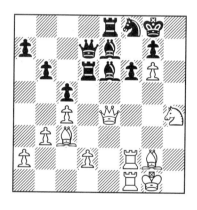 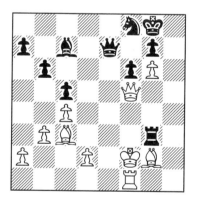

Diagram 31 (B)	Diagram 32 (B)
A thorn in Black's side	37 Bd5+ will be decisive

Breaking the pin with the deadly threat of 37 Bd5+, which is so strong that Black has nothing better than to give up the exchange with 36...Rxg2+.

36...Nd7? 37 Qd5+

The bishop check was still stronger, as 37 Bd5+! Kf8 38 Rh1! Qd6 39 Rh8+ Ke7 40 Qe4+ Ne5 41 Kxg3 wins the rook for free.

37...Kf8 38 Rh1 Rxg2+ 39 Qxg2

But the exchange is enough anyway, while Black still has problems with the g6-pawn creating mating nets.

39...Qe6 40 Qd5

Forcing Black to swap queens, after which the win is very straightforward.

40...Qxd5 41 cxd5 Bf4 42 Kf3 Bg5 43 Ke4 Ke7 44 Rh7 Bh6 45 Kf5 b5 46 d6+! 1-0

Game 22
□ G.Giorgadze ■ B.Kouatly
Manila Olympiad 1992

1 e4 c5 2 Nc3 e6 3 f4 d5 4 Nf3 dxe4 5 Nxe4 Nc6 (Diagram 33)

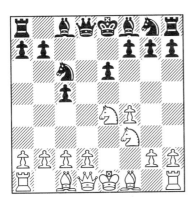 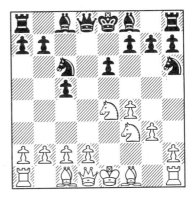

Diagram 33 (W)	Diagram 34 (W)
Black plays 5...Nc6	Black plays to control d4

The most natural and main move for Black.

6 g3

The old system was employed by Hebden and the other English players who popularized this variation. Instead:

a) 6 Bb5 is the main move nowadays, but it doesn't seem totally convincing for White: 6...Bd7 7 0-0 (7 Qe2 Qc7 8 0-0 0-0-0 9 d3 Nf6 10 Bd2 Nxe4 11 dxe4 Be7 12 c3 Kb8 13 Be3 f6 14 a3 Rhg8 15 b4 was good for White in G.Giorgadze-R.Cifuentes Parada, Spanish Team Championship 2002, but Black doesn't need to play so provocatively; 7...Nh6!?, planning ...Nf5, looks more sensible) 7...Nf6 8 Nxf6+ (this should probably be preferred to 8 d3 a6 9 Nxf6+ gxf6 10 Ba4 Nd4 11 Bxd7+ Qxd7 12 Be3 Nf5 13 Qe2 0-0-0 14 Bf2 Qc7 with a messy position, J.Polgar-V.Kramnik, Cap D'Agde rapid 2003) 8...gxf6!? (or 8...Qxf6 9 Ne5 Rc8! 10 Nxd7 Kxd7, M.Sadler-J.Lautier, Monte Carlo blindfold rapid 1998) 9 f5!? (9 b3 might be safer) 9...Qc7 is also very unclear but White's plan in G.Malbran-S.Mellano, Buenos Aires 1993, seems very odd: 10 fxe6 fxe6 11 Ne1?! Qe5 12 Qe2 Bd6 13 Qxe5 Bxe5 and Black was better if anyone.

b) 6 b3 is another possibility. White wants to get a typical double fianchetto position and elects to develop the dark-squared bishop first. For example, 6...Nf6 (Palliser suggests 6...Nh6!? again and, indeed, once White has committed himself to b2-b3 he won't want to play c2-c3 as well, so the d4-square will be vulnerable) 7 Nf2 Nd5 8 g3 Be7 9 Bb2 Bf6 10 Ne5 Qc7 11 Nfg4 Nxe5 12 fxe5 Be7 13 Bg2 h5 14 Nf2 Bd7 15 Qf3 Bc6 16 Ne4 Nb4 17 0-0 and White was better in J.Hickl-P.Cramling, Biel 1988.

6...Nf6

Black has tried several other moves:

a) 6...Be7 7 Bg2 Nf6 8 Nf2 0-0 9 b3 (the double fianchetto looks the most promising scheme; instead 9 0-0 Qc7 10 Qe2 b6 11 c3 Bb7 12 d3 Rad8 13 Be3 Rfe8 14 Rad1 Bf8 15 Bc1 g6 16 Rfe1 Bg7 saw Black employ it effectively, M.Todorcevic-L.Ljubojevic, Szirak Interzonal 1987) 9...Nd5 10 Bb2 Bf6 11 Ne5 Nxe5 12 fxe5 Be7 13 Ne4 with the better game, M.Hebden-O.Rodriguez Vargas, Malaga 1987.

b) 6...f5!? (a radical attempt to unbalance the position) 7 Nf2 Bd6 8 b3 Nh6 (if 8...e5 9 fxe5 Nxe5 10 Bb5+ Bd7 11 Bxd7+ Qxd7 12 Bb2 Nxf3+ 13 Qxf3 leaves White with a slight edge as now the f5-pawn looks a little weak) 9 Bb2 0-0 10 Bg2 Nf7 11 Nd3!, M.Hebden-Cu.Hansen, Malmo 1987, saw White bring all his pieces round to control the e5-square weakened by 6...f5.

c) 6...Nh6!? **(Diagram 34)** again heads to f5 to control the d4-square. Against this set-up, rather than fianchettoing the bishop on b2, I think playing d2-d3 and c3-c3 to control d4 seems more sensible; e.g. 7 Bg2 Be7 8 0-0 0-0 9 d3 Qd7 10 c3 Rd8 11 Ne5! Nxe5 12 fxe5 Qxd3 13 Bxh6 Qxd1 14 Raxd1 Rxd1 15 Rxd1 gxh6 16 Bf3 Rb8 17 Bh5 b6 18 Rf1 with a clear advantage, A.Cabrera-I.Teran Alvarez, Havana 1998.

7 Nxf6+

Normally the knight retreats to f2, but the text is an interesting idea by Giorgadze. White simply completes his development without worrying too much about how big his advantage will be out of the opening.

7...Qxf6 8 Bg2 g6 9 0-0 Bg7 10 d3 0-0 11 c3!

Controlling the d4-square and covering the b2-pawn, so that White can bring out his c1-bishop.

11...Qe7 12 Be3 Rd8 13 Qe2 (Diagram 35)

All White's pieces are developed and he stands slightly better. Black's bishop on c8 is still passive and lacks a good development square, while White can target the weak c5-pawn and use the e5-square as a useful outpost.

13...Bd7 14 Qf2 b6 15 Ne5!

Exploiting the pin on the long diagonal to claim the two bishops.

15...Rac8 16 Nxd7 Qxd7 17 Rad1 Ne7 18 g4!

 WARNING: g3-g4 is a move you have to be very careful about. Here it may look as though White is weakening his king, but Black's pieces aren't coordinated in such a way that he can exploit it, and it's important not to allow Black's knight the f5-square.

18...Qb5 19 Qe2 Rd6 20 Bf2 Rcd8 21 Bh4! (Diagram 36) **21...Re8 22 Bxe7**

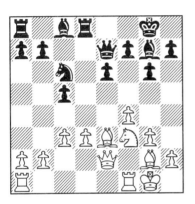

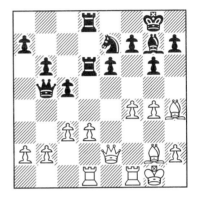

Diagram 35 (B)

White stands slightly better

Diagram 36 (W)

To remove the defending knight

Giving up the two bishops in order to start an offensive on the light squares.

22...Rxe7 23 f5

White continues to play very forcefully, continually creating threats for Black to deal with.

23...Red7 24 f6 Bh6 25 c4 Qa4 26 h4!?

Offering the a2-pawn which he considers to be of little importance, since White wants to mate!

26...Rd8

Giving a square for Black's queen to retreat back into the game. After 26...Qxa2 27 g5 Bf8 28 h5 Qb3 29 Be4 White has a huge initiative, while Black's extra pawn does not seem to change the assessment of the position.

27 Be4 Rd4 28 g5 Bf8 29 h5 (Diagram 37)

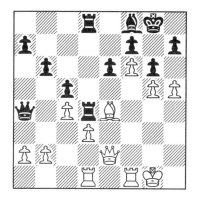

Diagram 37 (B)

The attack marches on

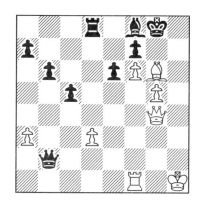

Diagram 38 (B)

The winning move

White's attack marches on.

29...Qd7 30 hxg6 hxg6 31 Qg4

Here White starts to lose total control of the position. Perhaps the simple 31 Kg2 was stronger, after which he can play Rh1 and mate Black down the h-file.

31...Qd6 32 Rd2?!

Losing the c4-pawn and suddenly the position is not clear. It would have been better first to reinforce his position with Kg2 and perhaps b2-b3, before continuing his attack with Qh4 and Rh1.

32...Rxc4 33 Rg2

Unfortunately, the desired 33 Rh2 runs into 33...Qxd3! 34 Qh4 Qe3+! 35 Kh1 Qxe4+, which stops White's mate and leaves Black with a decisive material advantage.

33...Rb4 34 a3 Qd4+ 35 Kh1 Rxb2?

Perhaps this was a time scramble as the text loses for Black. Instead, 35...Qxd3! leads to an unclear ending after 36 Bxd3 Rxg4 37 Rxg4 Rxd3.

36 Rxb2 Qxb2 37 Bxg6! (Diagram 38)

Now White is winning again, since 37...fxg6 38 Qxe6+ Kh8 39 Qh3+ Kg8 40 f7+ Kg7 41 Qh6 is mate.

37...Rd7 38 Be4

Black cannot stop the dual threats of Qh5 and g5-g6.

38...Rd4 39 g6 Bd6 40 gxf7+ Kxf7 41 Qg7+ 1-0

Conclusion

In my experience Black does not play 2...e6 very often against 2 Nc3, probably because Open Sicilians with an early ...e7-e6 are not as popular as those after 2...d6 or 2...Nc6. Nevertheless White has to learn the correct ideas to respond to Black's set-up. In the lines where Black plays an early ...a7-a6 White has no good square on the f1-a6 diagonal for his light-squared bishop, so he usually fianchettos it on g2. I believe the bishop is also better suited here against 3...d5, despite 6 Bb5 being more topical. In these lines White cannot generate such a quick attack on the black king, and so instead targets Black's centre, while building up on the kingside more slowly.

Chapter Five

Other Second Moves for Black

▨ **The First Few Moves**

▨ **Illustrative Games**

▨ **Conclusion**

The First Few Moves

In this chapter we will examine Black's remaining options after 2 Nc3, including all those variations in which he plays an early ...a7-a6.

1 e4 c5 2 Nc3 a6 (Diagram 1)

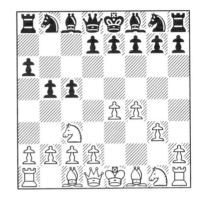

Diagram 1 (W)	Diagram 2 (B)
Black plans ...b7-b5	Position after 4 g3

A rare idea which I think is undervalued. Black is planning on a quick ...b7-b5 and possibly ...b5-b4, annoying the knight on c3 and interfering with White's development, before Black turns to the kingside himself.

The smaller queenside fianchetto, 2...b6!?, is considered in Game 26. The more standard kingside one normally transposes to main lines; i.e. 2...g6 3 f4 Bg7 4 Nf3 and then 4...d6 5 Bc4 Nc6 is Chapter Three, 4...Nc6 5 Bc4 or 5 Bb5 is Chapters One and Two, while 4...e6 5 d4! is the subject of Game 25.

3 f4 b5

Black's most independent approach. Naturally there are many different transpositions possible to normal second moves. In particular, 3...e6 4 Nf3 Nc6 transposes directly to the 4...a6 line in Chapter Four, while 4...d5 5 d3 will probably do so as well, since Black will have to play ...Nc6 at some point; for instance, 5...Nc6 6 g3 is Game 18, while 6 Be2 is Game 19.

Black can also hold back his queen's knight in favour of ...d7-d6. The line 3...d6 4 Nf3 b5 is covered (by transposition) in Game 24, while 3...e6 4 Nf3 d6 appears in the notes to the same game.

4 g3! (Diagram 2)

White prepares to reinforce his centre in readiness for Black's plan of ...Bb7, ...e7-e6 and ...d7-d5. The resulting positions are the subject of the first game below.

Illustrative Games

Game 23
☐ **P.Harikrishna** ■ **Bu Xiangzhi**
Tiayuan 2005

---

1 e4 c5 2 Nc3 a6 3 f4 b5

Black goes for immediate counterplay on the queenside. 3...d6 is considered in the next game.

4 g3!

I prefer this to the immediate 4 Nf3 as then 4...Bb7 **(Diagram 3)** creates a few problems for White:

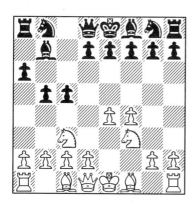

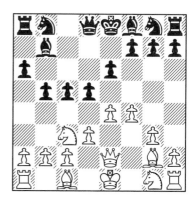

Diagram 3 (W)	**Diagram 4 (B)**
Black targets the e4-pawn	Overprotecting the e-pawn

5 d3 (5 Qe2 Nc6 6 d3 d6 7 Be3 e6 8 g4!? Nf6 9 g5 Nd7 10 Bh3 Nb6 11 f5 e5 was unclear in L.Aronian-L.Guidarelli, Bastia rapid 2003) 5...e6 6 g3 (6 Qe2 Nc6 7 g3 Nd4 8 Qf2 Nxf3+ 9 Qxf3 f5 gave Black good play in M.Archangelsky-D.Tyomkin, Montreal 2000) 6...d5 7 Bg2 (compare this with 7 Qe2! in the main game) 7...b4 is promising for Black, Se.Ivanov-V.Popov, St. Petersburg 2002.

4...Bb7 5 Bg2 e6 6 d3 d5

Instead:

a) 6...d6 7 Nf3 Nf6 8 0-0 Nc6 9 Qe2 Be7 10 Nd1 (with the idea of rerouting the knight to f2 for the g3-g4 break, and perhaps playing c2-c3 and d3-d4) 10...b4 (trying to prevent c2-c3) 11 Nf2 a5 12 Be3 Nd7 13 c3 bxc3 14 bxc3 0-0 15 Rfb1 (unusually White plays on the queenside trying to exploit the weaknesses Black has created, such as the b5-square and a5-pawn) 15...Ba6 16 Qd1 Rb8 17 d4 and White was slightly better in Zhang Zhong-Xu Jun, HeiBei 2001.

b) 6...Nf6 7 Nf3 d5 8 e5 Nfd7 9 0-0 g6 10 g4 Nc6 11 f5 h6 12 Bf4 Nb6 13 d4 Nc4 14 b3 cxd4 15 Ne2 Bc5 16 Nexd4 Nxd4 17 Nxd4 Na3 18 fxe6 fxe6 19 Be3 Qc7 20 Qd3 Qxe5 21 Qxg6+ Kd7 22 Rf7+ Kc8 23 Qd3 a5 24 Qc3 1-0 G.Jones-J.Ashwin, Yerevan 2007, was my recent last round game from the World Junior Championship.

7 Qe2! (Diagram 4)

Reinforcing the e4-pawn and allowing the c3-knight to drop back to d1 if attacked.

7...Nc6

Alternatively, Black can drive the knight away:

a) 7...b4 8 Nd1 dxe4 9 dxe4 Nf6 10 e5!? Bxg2 11 Qxg2 Nd5 12 Ne3 Nc6 13 Ne2 was E.Gasanov-A.Areshchenko, Ukrainian Junior Championships 2002. White has a slight advantage here as he can use the c4-square for his knight, leaving Black with a bad bishop as his c5-pawn hems it in. Realizing this, Black tried a dodgy pawn sacrifice with 13...c4?!, but I think he must have missed that after 14 Nxc4 Bc5 White has 15 Be3! with a clear advantage, as the knight will be hanging on c6 if the d5-knight moves.

b) 7...d4 8 Nd1 seems comfortable for White since, as we've seen in previous chapters, once Black has closed the centre White's attack on the kingside will be a lot stronger. A sample game ran 8...Nc6 9 Nf3 Nf6 10 0-0 Be7 11 Nf2 0-0 12 g4 c4!? (J.Houska-A.Kuzmin, Gibraltar 2004), and now White should accept the pawn, as I don't believe Black has enough compensation: 13 dxc4 bxc4 14 Qxc4 Rc8 15 Qe2 Nb4 16 Nxd4! Qxd4 17 c3 when White should retain the pawn with good chances.

8 Nf3

If 8 exd5 Nd4 and Black regains the pawn.

8...Nd4!?

Although this gives Black play down the semi-open c-file against c2, it also saddles him with a weak d4-pawn and a lack of pawn breaks. However, 8...Be7 9 0-0 Nf6 10 e5 Nd7, M.Kulesza-M.Adamski, Laczna 2002, and now 11 f5! would leave White with the edge.

9 Nxd4 cxd4 10 Nd1 dxe4

10...Bb4+ 11 Bd2 Bxd2+ 12 Qxd2 Qb6 13 0-0 Ne7 14 f5!? dxe4 15 dxe4 d3+ 16 Qe3 Qxe3+ 17 Nxe3 dxc2 18 Rac1 Rc8 19 Rf2 gave White a slight advantage, which he managed to convert in G.Giorgadze-M.Marin, Spanish Team Championship 2001.

11 dxe4 Rc8 12 0-0 (Diagram 5) 12...Nf6

12...Qc7!? might be Black's best try, trying to win the c2-pawn before White completes his development. After 13 Bd2!? (13 c3 dxc3 14 Nxc3 Nf6 is just equal) 13...Qxc2 (13...Nf6 14 Nf2 transposes to the next note; 13...Qc4!? might also be considered) 14 Rc1 Qa4 15 Nf2 White has good compensation with control of the c-file, better development and the useful e5-square for his knight; e.g. 15...Qxa2 16 Rxc8+ (16 e5!? Rxc1 17 Rxc1 Bxg2 18 Rc8+ Kd7 19 Rxf8 Bc6 is unclear) 16...Bxc8 17 Rc1.

13 Nf2 Be7

Now if 13...Qc7 14 Bd2 Qxc2 (or 14...Qc4 15 Nd3 Be7 16 Rfc1), then 15 e5! Nd5 (if 15...Bxg2? 16 Rfc1! skewers the queen and rook) 16 Bxd5 exd5 (not 16...Bxd5? 17 Rfc1 again) 17 Nd3 and White definitely has the better prospects.

14 b3

Developing the bishop on the long diagonal to target the weak d4-pawn.

14...0-0 15 Bb2 Qb6 16 Rad1

16 Rfd1 might be slightly more accurate.

16...Rfd8 17 Rd3 (Diagram 6)

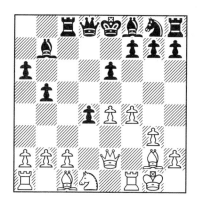

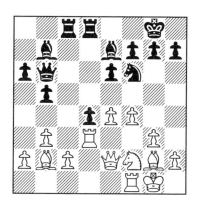

Diagram 5 (B)

Black should play on the c-file

Diagram 6 (B)

The pressure mounts on d4

Preparing to double on the d-file to increase the pressure on d4.

17...Qc7 18 Rc1 e5?!

This leads to the loss of the d4-pawn. 18...Bc5 would be better, but 19 Rcd1 gives White some advantage, as after 19...Bb6 20 Bxd4 Bxd4 21 Rxd4 Rxd4 22 Rxd4 Black cannot take the c-pawn due to 22...Qxc2?? 23 Qxc2 Rxc2 24 Rd8+ and mates.

19 fxe5 Qxe5 20 Rcd1

Black cannot defend d4, since if 20...Bc5 then 21 c3.

20...Qh5 21 Bf3 Qg6 22 Bxd4 (Diagram 7)

White is a pawn up and has a clear advantage.

22...Re8

22...b4, to clamp down a little on the white queenside, is probably Black's best try.

23 c3! Bf8 24 e5

Claiming more space and swapping off pieces to utilize his pawn advantage in the endgame.

24...Bxf3 25 Rxf3 Nd7 26 Nd3 Nc5 27 Nxc5 Bxc5 28 Bxc5 Rxc5 29 Rd7!

Targeting the f7-pawn.

29...Rf8 30 Rd6 Qh5 31 e6! (Diagram 8)

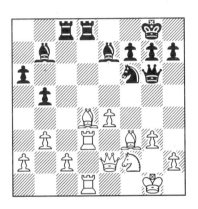

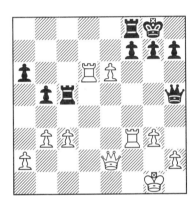

Diagram 7 (B)	Diagram 8 (B)
Black's d4-pawn has fallen	Simple, strong play

Simple, strong play by White.

31...Rc7?

31...fxe6? 32 Qxe6+ leads to mate, but 31...Re5 32 Qf1 f6 33 Rxa6 Re8 would put up more of a fight.

32 Rd7 Qc5+

If 32...Rxd7 33 exd7 wins.

33 Qe3 Qxe3+ 34 Rxe3 Rcc8 35 e7 Rfe8 36 Red3 1-0

Black has no defence to 37 Rd8 and 38 Rxc8 Rxc8 39 Rd8 etc.

Game 24
□ **E.Lobron** ■ **G.Andruet**
Marseilles 1989

---

1 e4 c5 2 Nc3 d6 3 f4 a6 4 Nf3 b5

On 4...e6 5 d3 Nc6 White can play 6 g4! with similar ideas to Game 20 in Chapter Four. Again he can get away with this early expansion as Black would have to waste a tempo to play ...d6-d5 and open the centre. B.Macieja-P.Jaracz, Polish Championship, Warsaw 2001, continued 6...b5 7 Bg2 Bb7 8 Qe2 Qc7 9 Be3 Nf6 10 g5 Nd7 11 0-0 and White was better with his space advantage on the kingside.

In another game GM Macieja went for 5 g4!? straight away, and after 5...d5 6 d3 Nf6 7 g5 dxe4 8 Ne5! Nfd7 9 Nxe4 Nxe5 10 fxe5 Qd4 11 Bg2 Nc6 12 c3 Qxe5 13 0-0 White had excellent compensation for the pawn, B.Macieja-R.Kempinski, Polish Championship, Plock 2000.

5 d4!? (Diagram 9)

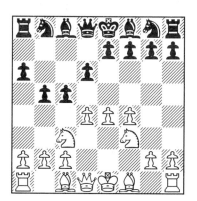

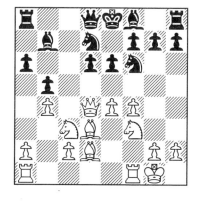

Diagram 9 (B)
White opens the Sicilian

Diagram 10 (B)
White has a safe edge

5 d3 Bb7 6 g3 e6 7 Bg2 is also possible, when we have a position similar to Game 23, albeit with the more restrained ...d7-d6 (rather than ...d7-d5). Instead White tries to exploit his opponent's lack of development by opening up the game.

5...cxd4 6 Qxd4 Bb7 7 Bd3

White develops his pieces normally and defends the e4-pawn, whereas Black has expanded on the queenside but is lagging behind badly on the kingside.

7...e6 8 Bd2 Nf6 9 0-0

White has completed his development and has a safe edge.

9...Nbd7 10 b4! (Diagram 10)

Grabbing space himself on the queenside, while stopping the black knight from jumping into c5.

10...Qb6 11 a4!

Now the a6 and b5-pawns start looking very shaky.

11...bxa4 12 Qxb6

12 Rxa4 looks more accurate, after which White can double on the a-file and should win the a6-pawn.

12...Nxb6 13 Be3 Rc8

Black misses his chance to get back into the game: 13...d5! and if 14 Bxb6 dxe4 regains the piece, while 14 e5 Ne4 is unclear.

14 Bxb6 Rxc3 15 Rxa4 Nxe4 16 b5! (Diagram 11)

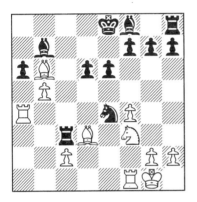

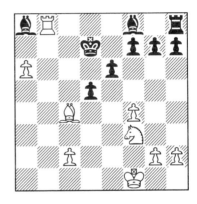

Diagram 11 (B)

A surprise double attack

Diagram 12 (B)

The a-pawn will promote

This unexpected double attack on the e4-knight and a6-pawn wins the game for White.

16...Nc5

16...axb5 also loses after 17 Ra7! Bc6 18 Rfa1! when Black cannot develop his kingside because of Ra8+, and otherwise White is simply winning, e.g. 18...d5 19 Rc7.

17 bxa6

17 Bxc5 Rxc5 18 bxa6 Ba8 19 Rb1 transposes to the game and cuts out a possibility for Black on his next move.

17...Ba8

Here 17...Bxf3 was a better defence, though White should still win after 18 Bb5+ Ke7 19 Rxf3! (19 Bxc5 Ba8 20 Ba3 Rxc2 is less clear) 19...Nxa4 20 Bxa4 Rc4 21 Bb5 Rxc2 22 a7 Ra2 23 Rc3 and 24 Rc8.

18 Bxc5 Rxc5 19 Rb1

White's a-pawn supported by all his pieces is simply too strong.

19...Rc8 20 Rc4 Rxc4

If 20...Rd8 21 Rc7 Be7 22 Rbb7! Bxb7 23 Bb5+ Kf8 24 axb7 g6 25 Rc8 Kg7 26 Bd7! wins.

21 Rb8+ Kd7 22 Bxc4 d5 23 Kf1! (Diagram 12) 1-0

Ruling out any ...Bc5+ tricks. Black resigned as he's unable to stop the a-pawn.

Game 25
☐ **E.Najer** ■ **V.Kron**
Moscow 1998

---

1 e4 c5 2 Nc3 g6

Now 3 d4 cxd4 4 Qxd4 Nf6 5 Nf3 Nc6 6 Qa4 d6 7 e5 gives White a fractional edge, but we'll stick to our Grand Prix scheme.

3 f4 Bg7 4 Nf3 e6 5 d4! (Diagram 13)

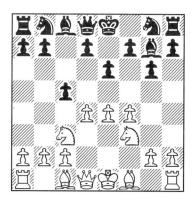 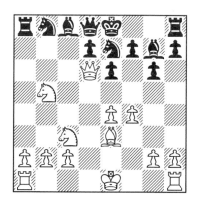

Diagram 13 (B)	Diagram 14 (B)
Opening the game again	Coming in on the dark squares

White opens up the game in order to play on the weakened dark squares. Black will always have to be careful as it is dubious to combine ...e7-e6 and ...g7-g6 in a mainline Sicilian, which is what we are transposing to.

5...cxd4 6 Nxd4 a6

Understandably, Black feels he must defend against Nc3-b5 and into d6. 6...Ne7 has also been played, when 7 Ndb5 d5 8 e5 0-0 seems ok for Black, but 7 Be3 d5 8 e5 Nbc6 9 Qd2 Bd7 10 Be2 Nxd4 11 Bxd4 Nf5 12 Bf2, as in Hol.Hernandez-G.Dominguez Aguilar, Merida 2003, gives White a pleasant advantage with his dark-square control and the possibilities of a kingside attack.

7 Be3 b5 8 Bxb5!?

An interesting piece sacrifice to exploit the weakness of d6. Otherwise 8 Qf3 Bb7 9

Bd3 is a typical Open Sicilian where White has the better chances thanks to his better development. He will castle queenside and start an offensive against the black king. The attack should be stronger than usual as Black has made weakening moves in front of his king, while White's pawns are all still on their starting squares.

8...axb5 9 Ndxb5 Ne7?!

Giving up another pawn with 9...d5 might be Black's best defence, although after 10 exd5 (10 Bd4!?) 10...Bxc3+ (not 10...exd5? 11 Nxd5 Na6 12 Bb6 and wins) 11 Nxc3 White's three pawns, lead in development, and play on the dark squares should be sufficient compensation for the piece.

10 Qd6! (Diagram 14)

White takes the d6 outpost for his queen and forces Black to give back material.

10...0-0

If 10...Ra6 11 Qxb8 or 10...Nbc6 11 Nc7+ wins.

11 Bb6 Nf5

Forced, since 11...Qe8? 12 Nc7 nets a whole rook.

12 exf5 Qh4+ 13 g3 Qh5 14 Bd4

14 fxg6 looks more accurate, when White's two pawn advantage should be enough to win the game.

14...Bxd4 15 Qxd4 Nc6 16 Qd2 Qxf5 17 Nd6 Qa5 (Diagram 15)

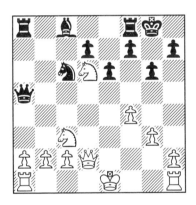

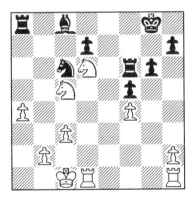

Diagram 15 (W)	**Diagram 16 (B)**
A great success for White	Black has no counterplay

White's opening has been a great success: he is a pawn up, while the great knight on d6 keeps Black from becoming active. He now wisely decides to swap queens to make use of his extra pawn and two connected passed pawns on the queenside.

18 Nce4 f5 19 Qxa5 Nxa5?!

19...Rxa5 would be a slight improvement.

20 Nc5! Nc6 21 c3

Stopping the black knight from jumping in to b4 or d4, and threatening to start advancing the a- and b-pawns. Meanwhile the white knights keep Black's pieces completely hemmed in.

21...e5 22 a4! exf4 23 gxf4 Rf6 24 0-0-0! (Diagram 16)

Denying Black any counterplay at all.

24...Nd8 25 b4 Ne6 26 Nxe6 Rxe6 27 Rhe1 Kf8 28 Rxe6 dxe6 29 Nxc8 Rxc8 30 Kc2

White has traded down to an easily winning rook endgame. His three connected passed pawns are simply too strong for Black to counter, who doesn't have any passed pawns at all.

30...Ke7 31 a5 g5 32 fxg5 e5 33 a6 Rb8 34 Ra1 Kd6 35 Ra5 f4 36 a7 Ra8 37 Kd3 f3 38 Ke3 e4 39 h4 1-0

Game 26
□ **A.Kosten** ■ **K.Arakhamia**
Aosta 1990

---

1 e4 c5 2 f4 b6!? 3 Nc3 Bb7 4 Nf3 Nf6

After 4...e6 5 d3 Be7 6 g3 (or 6 Be2!?) 6...Nc6 7 Bg2 we reach positions similar to those examined in Game 23, except that Black has played ...b7-b6 rather than ...a7-a6 and ...b7-b5. This should favour White, as the opposing counterplay on the queenside will be slower.

5 e5 Nd5 6 Bc4! (Diagram 17)

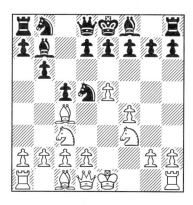

Diagram 17 (B)
Gaining time on the knight

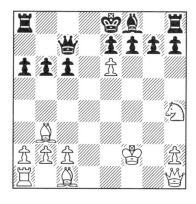

Diagram 18 (B)
White's forces are superior

White plays energetically against the black knight's early sortie and develops his pieces with gain of time.

6...e6

6...Nxf4 might be critical, but it looks very risky opening the f-file given White's lead in development. For example, 7 d4!? (7 0-0 e6 8 d4 transposes to the note to Black's 7th) and then:

a) 7...cxd4 8 Qxd4 Ng6 (8...Nxg2+ 9 Kf2 Nc6 10 Qe4 looks good for White as the knight on g2 is doomed) 9 e6!? dxe6 (or 9...fxe6 10 Qg4 Qc7 11 Bd3 with good compensation) 10 Qxd8+ Kxd8 11 Ng5 Ne5 12 0-0 and White will recapture at least a pawn, while Black's king is exposed in the middle and she will find it very difficult to develop her kingside.

b) 7...Nxg2+ 8 Kf2 Nh4 9 Nxh4 and here White's activity should make up for lack of king protection, as Black's pieces are a long way from drumming up any attack; e.g. 9...cxd4 10 Nb5 a6 11 Nxd4 Qc7 12 Bb3 Bxh1 13 Qxh1 Nc6 14 Nxc6 dxc6 15 e6 **(Diagram 18)**, when White retains a development and space advantage, while his two pieces are more useful here than Black's rook and two pawns.

7 0-0!?

7 Bxd5 exd5 8 d4 also leaves White with a comfortable advantage. 7 f5!? looks interesting too.

7...Be7

7...Nxf4 really has to be played now, but White's compensation isn't in doubt after 8 d4 cxd4 9 Nb5 Ng6 10 Nfxd4. Black can't take on e5 due to 10...Nxe5 11 Bf4! d6 12 Bxe5 dxe5 13 Qh5 and White's attack is too strong.

8 d4!

White correctly opens the position to utilize his lead in development and greater space.

8...0-0

8...Nxc3 9 bxc3 0-0 is answered by 10 d5 b5 11 Rb1!, leaving White with a clear advantage.

9 Nxd5 exd5 10 Bd3 (Diagram 19)

White has more space and a superior pawn structure, so should have all the chances. And as there's no longer a black pawn on e6 controlling f5, White's attacking prospects are increased, with f4-f5-f6 threatening to decimating the black kingside, .

10...c4 11 Be2 d6 12 c3 dxe5 13 dxe5

Obtaining the d4-outpost for his pieces, but giving Black counterplay. With hindsight 13 fxe5 is probably stronger, when White retains a safe advantage.

13...Bc5+ 14 Nd4 Nc6 15 Be3 f6 16 e6! (Diagram 20)

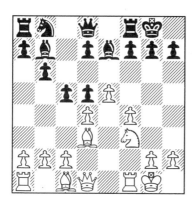

Diagram 19 (B)	Diagram 20 (B)
White has all the chances	Is the e-pawn weak or strong?

White has to be careful not to lose this pawn on e6, but taking on f6 would allow Black's pieces to coordinate; i.e. 16 exf6?! Qxf6 17 Qd2 Rae8 and Black is better here.

16...f5

Otherwise White plays f4-f5 himself, after which the pawn on e6 is very strong.

17 g4!?

White goes to drastic lengths to keep the e6-pawn.

17...Qd6 18 gxf5 Bxd4 19 Bxd4

19 cxd4 Ne7! is very unpleasant for White, so instead he gives up both f-pawns to keep the one on e6 with compensation.

19...Rxf5 20 Bg4 Rxf4 21 Qe2 Nxd4 22 cxd4 Re4

After 22...Rxd4 23 Rf7 Bc6 24 Raf1 Black is two pawns up, but White's rooks and advanced e-pawn give him very good play.

23 Qg2 Rf8 24 Rxf8+ Kxf8?!

24...Qxf8 25 Rf1 Rf4 looks a better way round for Black.

25 Rf1+ Rf4 26 Re1! (Diagram 21)

White is back on top. The e6-pawn has gone from being a potential weakness to a great strength, and Black has to be on the alert to stop it advancing further.

26...Qe7 27 Qg3 g5

Forced, as both 27...Rf6 28 Qb8+ and 27...Qg5 28 Qxf4+ Qxf4 29 e7+ Ke8 30 Bd7+ win at once.

28 h4

White uses all his pieces to attack and Black finds it very difficult to defend.

28...h6 29 hxg5 hxg5 30 Re5 Bc6?

After this Black has no way to defend her g5-pawn and once that drops her position collapses. 30...Kg7 was necessary, although White is still much better following 31 Bd1 Kh6 32 Bc2 Bc6 33 Qh3+ Rh4 34 Qf5 Be8 35 Rxd5.

31 Bh5! Rf6 32 Qxg5 Be8

If 32...Rxe6 33 Rf5+ leads to mate.

33 Rf5!

Swapping off the pieces so the e6-pawn becomes even stronger.

33...Rxf5 34 Qxf5+ Kg7 35 Bxe8 Qxe8 36 Qe5+ Kh6 37 e7 Kh7 38 Qe6 Kg7 39 Kg2 (Diagram 22) 1-0

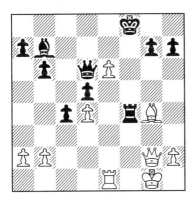

Diagram 21 (B)

The e-pawn is strong!

Diagram 22 (B)

Black will lose all her pawns

Black resigned as she can do nothing to prevent the white king coming up the board and taking all her pawns.

Conclusion

Black's most important deviations in this chapter are those with an early ...a7-a6. By expanding quickly on the queenside he prevents White's favoured set-up, but in doing so delays his own development and White should try to exploit this. I think these ...a7-a6 lines are underestimated and it's important as White to know a good move order to try and retain some advantage. Of the rest, 2...g6 will normally transpose to the main lines of the earlier chapters. 2...b6 is extremely rare, but it's an interesting option which shouldn't be dismissed immediately.

Chapter Six

2...Nc6 3 Bb5: Introduction

 The First Few Moves

Illustrative Games

Conclusion

The First Few Moves

1 e4 c5 2 Nc3 Nc6 3 Bb5 (Diagram 1)

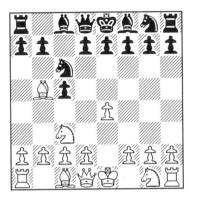

Diagram 1 (B)

White plays 3 Bb5

Diagram 2 (B)

Position after 5 f4

3 Bb5 is a sideline which has grown in popularity in the last few years. White's main aim is to reach a Grand Prix type position, but having swapped off his light-squared bishop, which is often a target for Black's counterplay, while damaging Black's queenside pawn structure. The position is similar to the Rossolimo, 1 e4 c5 2 Nf3 Nc6 3 Bb5, with two important differences: White has not yet played Ng1-f3 and so is able to get his attack going straight away with f2-f4; on the other hand the d4-square is now available for the black knight.

I have played 3 Bb5 as my main weapon against the Sicilian for many years, ever since being taught the line by my former coach IM Angus Dunnington. The most critical reply, 3...Nd4, is the subject of the next chapter, while all other third moves for Black are covered here.

3...g6

Against both 3...e6 and 3...d6 White can adopt a similar strategy. 3...a6? is just a waste of time as White was planning to take the knight on c6 anyway. However, 3...Na5!? is more sensible than it looks. Black doesn't mind losing a tempo with his knight as he plans to regain it attacking White's bishop. This move will be examined in Game 31.

4 Bxc6!

By swapping his bishop for the knight White leaves his opponent with a compromised pawn structure.

4...bxc6

If Black recaptures with the d-pawn (see Games 29 and 30) his counterplay will be much slower, as the ...b5-b4 push would leave c5 horribly exposed.

5 f4 (Diagram 2)

White continues in the normal theme of the Grand Prix Attack. If Black succeeds in stopping the kingside attack, White can often change tack and target the weak queenside pawns, in particular the one on c5, with a plan such as b2-b3, Ba3 and Na4.

5...Bg7 6 d3

It's a good idea to play an early d2-d3 as otherwise Black may try for ...c5-c4, impeding White's queenside development.

6...d6 7 Nf3 Nf6 8 0-0 Bg4 9 Qe1 Bxf3 10 Rxf3 0-0 11 Qh4 (Diagram 3)

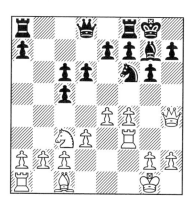
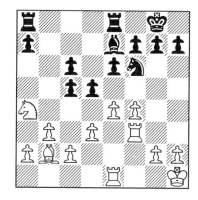

Diagram 3 (B)	Diagram 4 (B)
White has a big initiative	White is clearly better

White has quickly gained a big initiative on the kingside, while Black has not even started any counterplay. This plan of White's is very simple and effective and can be adopted against most of Black's defensive attempts, such as 8...0-0 9 Qe1 Ne8 and 6...Nh6 7 f4 0-0 in the first two games below.

Statistics

White has scored well in this line: 58%, with 1009 wins and 643 losses in 2262 games against a similar average rating. In recent games between top players, White's score has been even higher: 63%, with 26 wins and just 11 losses from 60 games in my database.

Illustrative Games

Game 27
☐ **Gil.Hernandez** ■ **C.Minzer**
Mislata 2000

---

1 e4 c5 2 Nc3 Nc6 3 Bb5 g6

Instead, G.Jones-C.Duggan, Cork 2006, saw 3...d6 4 Bxc6+ bxc6 5 f4, and here my opponent decided that ...d5 was the most sensible try for counterplay despite having spent a tempo on ...d6 already: 5...d5 6 d3 Nf6 7 Nf3 Bg4 8 0-0 e6 9 Kh1 (simply sidestepping any tactics on the g1-a7 diagonal) 9...Be7 (if 9...dxe4 10 dxe4 Qxd1 11 Rxd1 gives White a clear advantage) 10 Qe1 Bxf3 (otherwise 10...0-0 11 Ne5!) 11 Rxf3 0-0 12 b3! (Black's king is reasonably safe so I simply played against the weak c5-pawn) 12...Qa5 13 Bb2 Rfe8 14 Na4 Qxe1+ 15 Rxe1 **(Diagram 4)**. Black has succeeded in reaching a queenless middlegame but is clearly worse here with the huge weakness on c5, more cramped position and inferior bishop. Now Black didn't fancy letting me play c2-c4, fixing the weakness on c5, so he activated his bishop and tried to force some concessions in return for the pawn: 15...c4!? 16 bxc4 dxc4 17 Bxf6! (the white knight will be better than the bishop due to the holes in Black's position) 17...Bxf6 18 e5 Be7 19 dxc4 Rab8 20 Rb3 Rxb3 21 axb3 Rd8 22 Nc3 Bb4 23 Rd1 Rxd1+ 24 Nxd1 Bd2 25 g3 g5 26 fxg5 Bxg5 27 Kg2 Kg7 28 Kf3 Kg6 29 Ke4 and White won.

4 Bxc6 bxc6

The alternative recapture, 4...dxc6, is examined in Games 29 and 30.

5 f4 Bg7 6 Nf3 d6 7 0-0 Nf6 (Diagram 5)

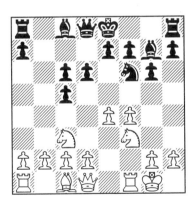

Diagram 5 (W)

Black soon gets into trouble

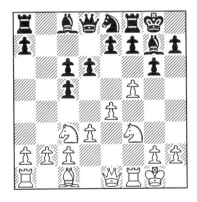

Diagram 6 (B)

The usual attacking thrust

Black develops his kingside logically but soon gets into trouble.

8 d3 0-0 9 Qe1

With the familiar plan of a quick assault on the black king. If Black does nothing White would play Qh4, f4-f5, Bh6, Ng5, and then try to get rid of the black knight on f6 with an exchange sacrifice or e4-e5 push.

9...Ne8

Removing the knight from being attacked by an e4-e5 break.

10 f5! (Diagram 6)

Offering a pawn to open up lines towards the black king. After 10...gxf5 11 Qh4! White has a lot of compensation: he will continue with Bh6 and Ng5 and the mating attack will be very difficult to stop. Therefore Black declines the pawn but still ends up in a lot of trouble.

The alternative was 10 Qh4!?, again threatening Black's weak king, but f4-f5 immediately is probably slightly more accurate.

10...e6 11 fxg6 hxg6

11...fxg6 is also met by 12 e5! d5 (after 12...dxe5 13 Ne4 Black may be a pawn up but c5 will drop quickly and the black pieces – the bishops in particular – are atrociously placed with no way of untangling them, while White can develop his remaining pieces and pick off the black pawns at will) 13 Na4! c4 14 Bg5 Qc7 15 d4, when White has an almost decisive advantage due to his better developed and more active pieces, more space and a superior pawn structure. It will be almost impossible to dislodge the knight from c5, while the black bishops again look like very sorry pieces.

12 e5! (Diagram 7)

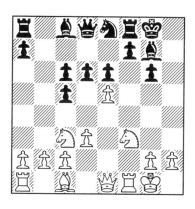

Diagram 7 (B)

A positional pawn sacrifice

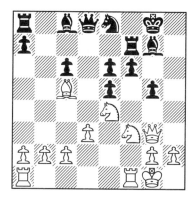

Diagram 8 (B)

Black's position is abysmal

White plays another temporary pawn sacrifice, but this one is positional. Black's pieces are now forced to remain passive and his pawn structure is shattered.

12...dxe5

If 12...d5 13 Na4 c4 14 d4 and Black's position is again very miserable.

13 Be3 f6

Black tries to defend at least one of his pawns and uses an unorthodox set-up to develop his f8-rook. If instead 13...Qa5 then 14 Qf2 and the c5-pawn will drop.

14 Bxc5 Rf7 15 Qg3

Unfortunately 13...f6 weakened another pawn, namely the one on g6, so White targets it and forces further positional weaknesses.

15...g5 16 Ne4 (Diagram 8)

The position is already abysmal for Black: his bishop on g7 is blocked in by his own pawns, his rook on a8 is still undeveloped, as is the bishop on c8, which is also blocked in by pawns.

16...Qc7 17 Rf2!

White calmly doubles rooks on the f-file, while Black is unable to do anything active. It says something that *Fritz's* suggestion here is 17...Qd8.

17...Bf8 18 Nfxg5!

White sacrifices a knight to blow open the kingside. All of his pieces (apart from the rook at a1 which will come to f1 shortly) are looking towards the enemy king, while Black's rook on a8 and bishop on c8 have no role at all.

18...Bxc5

Now White just continues his attack with a material plus. Black had to try 18...fxg5, though White has several wins, the simplest being 19 Bxf8 Kxf8 (19...Rxf8 20 Rxf8+ Kxf8 21 Rf1+ transposes, and 19...Rxf2 20 Qxf2 Qf7 21 Rf1 is hardly any better) 20 Rxf7+ Kxf7 (if 20...Qxf7 21 Rf1) 21 Rf1+ Kg8 (21...Ke7 22 Qxg5+ Kd7 23 Rf7 is mate) 22 Qxg5+ Qg7 23 Qh5 Bb7 24 Rf3 and 25 Rg3 picks up the queen.

19 Nxf7+ Kxf7 20 Nxc5 (Diagram 9)

White is the exchange and a pawn up and still holds all the trumps. Black could resign here quite comfortably but tries to make the game a respectable length.

20...Rb8 21 b3 Rb4 22 Ne4 f5 23 c4 Rb7 24 Ng5+ Kf8 25 Nf3 e4 26 Qxc7 Rxc7 27 dxe4 Nf6 28 exf5 exf5 29 Rd1 1-0

Game 28
☐ **G.Jones** ■ **D.Stojanovski**
Pula 2007

---

1 e4 c5 2 Nc3 Nc6 3 Bb5 g6 4 Bxc6 bxc6 5 f4 Bg7 6 Nf3 Nh6!?

Played quickly by my opponent so maybe it was preparation, though White has a very nice edge in this position.

7 d3 0-0 (Diagram 10) 8 f5?!

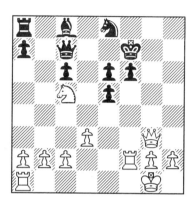

Diagram 9 (B)

White is winning easily

Diagram 10 (W)

White has a nice edge

In order to rule out ...f7-f5 and continue my attack. However, 8 0-0 f5 leaves White with a pleasant advantage. Although Black has prevented f4-f5, he has also weakened himself, and after 9 e5 his pieces look rather strangely placed – in particular, neither of his bishops has good prospects – and he has weak c-pawns. White can continue with normal moves such as Na4, b2-b3 and Bb2 or Ba3 (and maybe c2-c4) to attack c5, whereas Black is in a bind without an easy plan and will find it hard to activate his pieces.

8...d5

If 8...gxf5 9 Nh4 fxe4 10 Qh5 and Black's knight on h6 is embarrassingly short of squares.

9 fxg6 fxg6

After 9...hxg6 10 0-0 White has an even stronger attack than normal with Qe1-h4 and Ng5 coming swiftly.

10 0-0 Nf7

Black tries to bring his offside knight back into the game.

11 Qe1

Now as well as the usual plan of Qh4 (or Qg3), White can consider playing e4-e5, blocking in the black bishop on g7 and knight on f7.

11...c4!? (Diagram 11)

Black takes drastic action to try and get some queenside counterplay and improve his pawn structure.

12 dxc4

Not 12 d4?! e5 and Black equalizes as he contests the centre.

12...dxc4?

I really didn't understand this move my opponent blitzed out. I presumed the idea of 11...c4 was 12...Ba6, to retake the pawn with the bishop (e.g. 13 Rf2 Bxc4), while White cannot capture on d5 due to the pin against the f1-rook.

> **WARNING: My idea was to play 13 e5 Bxc4 14 Rf2 with the plan of b2-b3, Na4 and Bb2 or Ba3, after which I would have nice outposts at c5 and d4 for my knights, while Black's pieces lack good squares. However, I underestimated the temporary piece sacrifice 14...Nxe5!! 15 Nxe5 Rxf2 16 Kxf2 Qb6+ 17 Be3 Qxb2, when White has to return the piece with interest.**

Therefore White has to be content with 13 Nd2 **(Diagram 12)**, simply defending the c4-pawn, so that if Black wants material equality he will have to wreck his pawn structure again. For example:

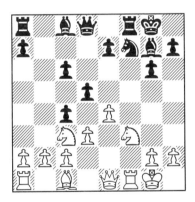

Diagram 11 (W)

Trying for counterplay

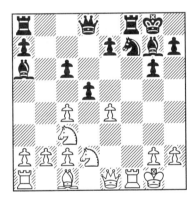

Diagram 12 (B)

Position after 13 Nd2

a) 13...Qb6+ 14 Kh1 d4 (after 14...Bxc4 15 Nxc4 dxc4 16 Rb1 White has a nice edge with the superior pawn structure, so Black goes for the initiative) 15 Na4 Qa5 16 b3 and I think White stands better, a pawn up for minimal compensation; e.g. 16...d3 17 Bb2! Bxb2 18 Nxb2 dxc2 19 Qc1 Qc3 20 Na4 and White regains the pawn with a beautiful position, since if 20...Qd3? 21 Nc5.

b) 13...e6 is less clear: although a pawn up White has a little trouble completing his development, while Black is quite active here. If White doesn't wish to relinquish the initiative he should prefer 8 0-0 to 8 f5.

13 Qg3

I wanted to play 13 Qh4 but thought 13...h6 was rather annoying, so instead I put the queen on g3 where it covers the b8-square, with the idea of simply completing my development.

13...Qa5 14 Be3 Bxc3?!

This gives White too much play on the dark squares towards the black king, but the position was already horrible for Black. He has an awful pawn structure and no good square for his light-squared bishop, while White can start his kingside attack with either Bd4 or Ng5.

15 bxc3 Qxc3 16 Bd4 Qxc2? (Diagram 13)

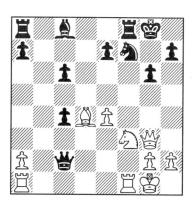

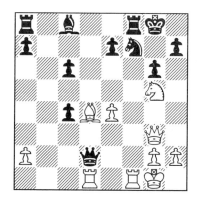

Diagram 13 (W)
White has a choice of wins

Diagram 14 (B)
A decisive intermezzo

And this move loses as the queen is now too far offside. Either 16...Qa5 or 16...Qa3 was forced, but White has a huge attack for the pawn – and even if Black eventually fights it off, he would still be worse in the ending despite his pawn advantage because of his hideous structure.

17 Ng5

I saw lots of pretty lines here, exploiting the fact that Black's queen, a8-rook and bishop are all out of the game. 17 Ne5 also wins (e.g. 17...Qxe4 18 Rf4! Qc2 19 Nxf7 Rxf7 20 Rxf7 Kxf7 21 Qe5!), but it seemed safer to cover the e4-pawn and make sure the black queen stayed out of play.

17...Qd2

Instead:

a) 17...Nxg5 18 Qe5 Rf6 19 Qxe7 wins.

b) 17...Qd3 18 Qf2 forces Black to give up a piece with 18...Bf5 19 Nxf7 Rxf7 20 exf5.

c) 17...c5, trying to knock the bishop off the a1-h8 diagonal, doesn't achieve anything after 18 Bc3! – though at the time I was looking at the pretty 18 Nxh7!, when 18...Qxe4 (if 18...Kxh7 19 Rxf7+ Rxf7 20 Qh4+ Kg8 21 Qh8 mate, or 18...cxd4 19 Qxg6+ Kh8 20 Nxf8 and mates on h7) 19 Nxf8 Qxd4+ 20 Kh1 Qg4 (if 20...Kxf8 21 Qf3 hits f7 and a8) 21 Qxg4 Bxg4 22 Nxg6 Be2 (if 22...e5 23 Rxf7!) 23 Nxe7+ Kf8 24 Rf2 leaves White the exchange up and he should win.

18 Rad1! (Diagram 14)

My opponent missed this move, defending the d4-bishop, while the knight on g5 still can't be taken: 18...Qxg5 19 Rxf7! Qxg3 20 Rg7+ Kh8 21 Rxe7+ (not yet 21 Rxg6+??, because of 21...e5! and Black wins) 21...Kg8 22 Rg7+ (an amusing manoeuvre) 22...Kh8 23 Rxg6+ Rf6 24 Bxf6 mate.

18...Qa5 19 Nxf7

Simply swapping off the pieces defending Black's king.

19...Rxf7 20 Rxf7 Kxf7 21 Qf4+ Ke8

If 21...Kg8 22 Qh6 e5 23 Bxe5 Qxe5 24 Rd8+ Kf7 25 Qf8+ Ke6 26 Re8+ wins. 21...Ke6 is forced, but it looks extremely ugly and White should be able to win easily with Black's pieces so dispersed. *Fritz* suggests the slightly strange 22 Bh8!, opening the d-file for the rook; e.g. 22...Ba6 23 Qg4+ Kf7 24 Rf1+ Kg8 25 Bd4 Bc8 26 Qf4 or 22...Qc5+ 23 Kh1 Ba6 24 Qg4+ Kf7 25 Bd4 Qd6 26 Ba1 Qc5 27 Rf1+ Ke8 28 Bg7! and wins.

22 Bg7! (Diagram 15)

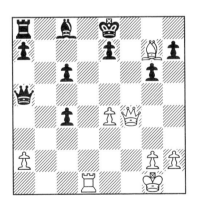 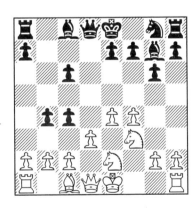

Diagram 15 (B)

The black king is surrounded

Diagram 16 (W)

A suspicious counterattack

Threatening Qf8 mate.

22...Qc5+ 23 Kh1 e5 24 Qf6 Bg4

Or 24...Qe7 25 Qxc6+ and Black drops the rook.

25 Rd6! 1-0

Completing the net by cutting off the queen on c5 from defending the f8-square, so mate or large loss of material is unavoidable.

Game 29
□ **G.Jones** ■ **G.Eppinger**
Calvia 2006

1 e4 c5 2 Nc3 Nc6 3 Bb5 g6 4 Bxc6 dxc6 5 f4

In the next game White plays 5 d3 first, which may be slightly more accurate as it discourages ...c5-c4 ideas.

5...Bg7 6 Nf3 b5?!

Rather than allow White's swift kingside assault, Black tries for an immediate attack on the queenside, but this leaves c5 very weak.

 WARNING: Be very careful when advancing like this, as it leaves the c5-pawn no longer able to be defended by another pawn.

7 d3 b4 8 Ne2 c4!? (Diagram 16)

My opponent played these moves very quickly as though it was all preparation, and indeed, when I put this on *Fritz* it thought it was equal! In fact, White will have a clear advantage due to Black's hideous queenside pawn structure.

9 dxc4 Qxd1+ 10 Kxd1 Ba6 11 a3! bxa3 12 Rxa3 Bxc4 13 b3 Be6 14 Be3 (Diagram 17)

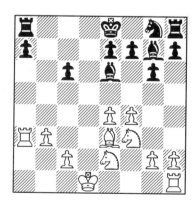

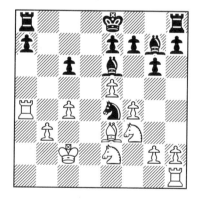

Diagram 17 (B)
Black is left with weak pawns

Diagram 18 (B)
Planning to double on the a-file

The dust has settled on the queenside. Black has managed to regain his sacrificed pawn, but in the process has been left with weak a- and c-pawns, while White has a lead in development. Furthermore, with the queens exchanged the king on d1 is an active piece rather than a liability, and White can quickly target Black's weaknesses.

14...Nf6 15 e5!

Shutting the bishop in on g7. It will take Black a long time to get that piece back in the game.

15...Ne4

The knight jumps into the centre of the board, a nice outpost, but it has nowhere to go from there. On the other hand, there is hardly anything better: 15...Nd5 16 Bc5 and the knight will be driven back with c2-c4, or 15...Ng4 16 Bc5 and h2-h3 will follow, while 15...Nd7 meets with 16 Ned4.

16 Ra4!

Forcing Black to make a decision.

16...Bd5

16...f5 is the other way to defend the knight, but that would leave the bishop trapped on g7 for the rest of the game.

17 c4 Be6 18 Kc2 (Diagram 18)

White has gained two tempi on the black bishop and now threatens to play Rha1 to win the a-pawn, which Black cannot prevent.

18...f6 19 Ned4!

Winning the c-pawn, as 19...Bd7 allows 20 e6.

19...Bg4 20 Nxc6 a6 21 Rha1 Bc8 22 b4 Kf7 23 Nfd4 (Diagram 19) 1-0

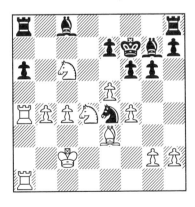

Diagram 19 (B)

Black is completely lost

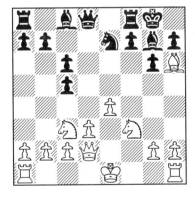

Diagram 20 (B)

White will castle long

Black is only one pawn down but, apart from the knight on e4, his pieces are passive and useless. Once White wins the a-pawn as well, the passed b- and c-pawns will decide the game. Therefore Black decided to end the misery and resigned.

Game 30
☐ B.Macieja ■ K.Haznedaroglu
European Championship, Antalya 2004

1 e4 c5 2 Nc3 Nc6 3 Bb5 g6 4 Bxc6 dxc6 5 d3

An alternative to 5 f4 in the previous game, intending to follow with f2-f4.

5...e5

Rather than allowing White's easy plan, Black tries to deter the f-pawn's advance.

6 f4!

Macieja plays it anyway!

6...exf4 7 Bxf4 Bg7 8 Nf3 Ne7 9 Qd2 0-0 10 Bh6!? (Diagram 20)

10 0-0 is also possible, but White decides that his attack will be much faster than Black's, so he can afford to castle queenside.

10...Bg4 11 0-0-0 b5 12 h3 Be6

After 12...Bxf3 13 gxf3 Black has not got far with his attack, whereas White has the simple plan of h4-h5 to open the h-file and would win quickly.

13 h4 Bg4

Haznedaroglu tries to stop the h4-h5 break, but this allows...

14 Bxg7 Kxg7 15 Qf4! (Diagram 21)

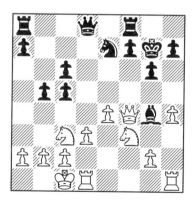

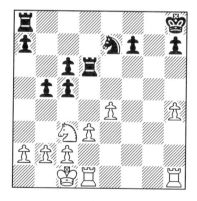

Diagram 21 (B)	Diagram 22 (W)
Forcing concessions	White has a good endgame

15...Bxf3

Black is now forced to take the knight, since if the bishop retreats 16 h5 would be very strong, while 15...h5 drops the c5-pawn after 16 Qe5+.

16 gxf3 Qb8 17 Qe3

White doesn't want to trade queens as his attack would then be diminished.

17...Qe5 18 f4 Qd4

Black desperately hopes for a queen swap to relieve the pressure, but Macieja merely sidesteps.

19 Qg3 Rg8 20 f5 Kh8 21 fxg6 Rxg6 22 Qc7 Qd6 23 Qxd6 Rxd6 (Diagram 22)

Having forced a positional concession, Macieja doesn't mind trading into a very favourable endgame. His pieces are more active and he has a much better pawn structure with two pawn islands to Black's three. The doubled pawns on the c-file add to Black's misery.

24 Rdf1 Rf8 25 Rf4!

Threatening to double on the f-file to target the weak f-pawn.

25...f5 26 Rhf1 Rdf6 27 Ne2!

The knight heads over to g3 to join the offensive against the f-pawn.

27...Ng6

If 27...Kg7 28 Ng3 fxe4 29 Nh5+ wins.

28 Rxf5 Rxf5 29 exf5 Nxh4 30 Ng3

Black has managed to trade his weak f-pawn for the h-pawn, but now White has an advanced passed pawn and the nice e4-square for his knight.

30...Rg8 31 Ne4 Rg4 32 f6 Ng6 33 Rf5 (Diagram 23)

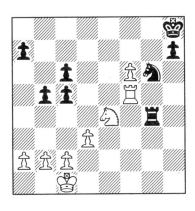

Diagram 23 (B)

Attacking the weak pawns

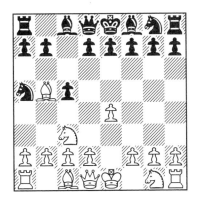

Diagram 24 (W)

Black plays 3...Na5!?

There's no need to move the knight from its solid outpost. Instead, White brings his rook into play, attacking the weak queenside pawns.

33...c4 34 Rc5 cxd3 35 cxd3 Kg8 36 Rxc6

White infiltrates with his rook and wins a pawn. With the protected knight on e4 guarding the strong passed f-pawn, the rest of the game is easy.

36...Ne5 37 Rc8+ Kf7 38 Kd2 Rg2+ 39 Kc3 Rg1 40 Rc7+ Ke6 41 Rxh7 a5 42 Kd4 Nc6+ 43 Kc5 1-0

Game 31
☐ G.Jones ■ Ad.Horvath
European Club Cup, Fuegen 2006

---

1 e4 c5 2 Nc3 Nc6 3 Bb5 Na5!? (Diagram 24) 4 Nf3

Against 3...Na5, rather than continuing with the Grand Prix theme, I advise playing differently. With 4 Nf3 White simply wants to play in Open Sicilian style, trying to take advantage of Black's numerous knight moves.

Nevertheless, 4 f4 is also possible, when 4...a6 5 Be2 reaches positions similar to those in Game 19. In fact 5...e6 6 Nf3 d5 7 d3 is identical, except that the black knight on a5 rather than c6.

4...a6 5 Be2 b5 6 d4

Transposing into an Open Sicilian type position. White has taken two tempi to bring his bishop to e2, but it can be argued that the black knight is somewhat offside on a5 now.

6...cxd4 7 Nxd4 e6

After 7...b4 there is the curious line 8 Nd5! e6 9 Bg5!!. Black cannot take the bishop as Nc7+ would pick up the rook, so 9...f6 is forced, but after 10 Bh5+ g6 11 Nxf6+! Nxf6 12 Nxe6!? (otherwise 12 e5 Be7 13 exf6 Bxf6 14 Bf3 d5 15 Bxf6 Qxf6 16 0-0 with a slight advantage) 12...dxe6 13 Qxd8+ Kxd8 14 Bxf6+ Ke8 15 Bxh8 gxh5 White stands better with rook and two pawns vs. bishop and knight, as well as having the superior pawn structure.

8 a3

Cutting out any ...b5-b4 annoyances.

8...Bb7 9 0-0 (Diagram 25)

This game was played for Slough Sharks in the European Club Cup. I was on board one and at about this point went to look at the other games in the match. On board three I found they had exactly the same position! Only here did we vary: my opponent fell for a nice tactic and, seeing this, Black on board three decided to try something else.

9...d6?

The other game continued 9...Rc8 10 Be3 (this encourages ...Nc4; I prefer leaving the bishop on c1 and perhaps playing for f2-f4) 10...d6 11 Qe1 Nf6 12 f3 Be7 13 Rd1 Qc7 14 Ndxb5!? (14 Qg3 still promised White some advantage) 14...axb5 15 Nxb5 Qd8 16 e5 Nd5 17 exd6 Bf6 18 Rxd5? (there was no need for this; White should just play 18 Nc7+ as 18...Nxc7?? would lose to 19 d7+) 18...Bxd5 19 Nc7+ Rxc7 20 dxc7 Qxc7 21 Qb4 Nc6 22 Qa4? (22 Bb5 keeps White in the game) 22...0-0 23 c4 Qe5 24 cxd5 Qxe3+ 25 Kh1 0-1 G.Kafka-Ta.Horvath, European Club Cup, Fuegen 2006.

10 Ncxb5!

Exploiting Black's lack of development and the offside nature of his knight. If 10...axb5 11 Bxb5+ Ke7 12 b4 regains the piece and leaves White with a decisive advantage, a pawn up with Black's king stranded in the centre of the board.

10...Nf6

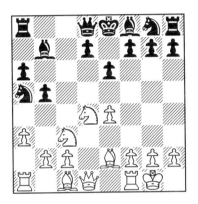

Diagram 25 (B)

An unusual Open Sicilian

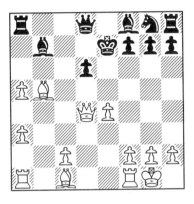

Diagram 26 (B)

White is winning

Black ignores my knight and tries to castle as quickly as possible. If instead 10...e5 11 b4! exd4 12 bxa5 axb5 13 Bxb5+ Ke7 14 Qxd4 **(Diagram 26)** would have given me huge compensation for the piece, as Black's king is stuck in the centre and he has no sensible way of developing his kingside. In fact *Fritz9* evaluates this position as winning for White already; one sample line could go 14...Qxa5 15 a4 Nf6 16 Ba3 Kd8 (16...Rd8 17 Qe5 mate would be rather embarrassing) 17 e5 Nd7 18 Bxd6 Bxd6 19 exd6 Rg8 20 Rfe1 Ba6 21 Bxd7 Kxd7 22 Re7+ Kd8 23 Re5 and wins.

11 Bg5 Be7

Again the lines after 11...axb5 12 Bxb5+ or 11...e5 12 b4 are not advisable for Black.

12 b4!?

Here 12 Nc3 Nxe4 13 Bxe7 Qxe7 14 Nxe4 Bxe4 15 Qd2 offers White a safe edge, but I was after more.

12...Nxe4

If 12...0-0 13 Nc3 Qc7 14 Na4 Nc6 15 f3 Nxd4 16 Qxd4 Qxc2 17 Nc3 is a little awkward for Black.

13 Bxe7 Qxe7 14 f3

Trading the knights on a5 and b5 will leave some holes on c5 and c3, so White forces the e4-knight to retreat first.

14...Nf6 15 bxa5 axb5 16 Bxb5+ Kf8 17 Qd2 (Diagram 27)

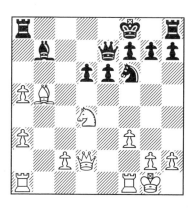

Diagram 27 (B)	Diagram 28 (W)
White is a pawn up	White to play and win

The dust has settled somewhat and we find White is a pawn up with better development, while it will take some time for Black to activate his h8-rook. The only positive in Black's position is his good pawn structure.

17...Qc7 18 Rfe1

Threatening Rxe6, or if 18...Qxa5 19 Nxe6+! fxe6 20 Qxd6+ Kf7 21 Qxe6+ gives White three pawns for the piece and a very strong attack; e.g. 21...Kg6 22 Bd3+ Kh6 23 Re5 Bc8 24 Qd6 Qc3 25 g4! threatening Rh5 mate.

18...Kg8 19 Nb3 h5

Black endeavours to develop his rook.

20 Rad1 Bd5

20...d5 would block Black's light-squared bishop and give White the c5-square.

21 Qd3

Threatening c2-c4 to win the d6-pawn, while stopping Black from playing ...Kh7 to help develop that h8-rook.

21...Qa7+

21...Bxb3 22 cxb3 Rxa5 would regain the pawn, but then White has two dangerous connected passed pawns, while Black still has to complete development.

22 Qd4

I don't mind swapping queens as d6 is so weak.

22...Bxb3 23 Qxa7 Rxa7 24 cxb3 Rxa5 25 a4 Nd5 (Diagram 28)

25...d5 might be a better try, but my queenside pawns should settle the game, as Black cannot then bring his knight across to help impede their progress.

26 Rxd5!

Removing Black's best defender and swapping off into an easily won endgame.

26...exd5 27 Re8+! Kh7 28 Rxh8+ Kxh8

Black is now the exchange up, but the two connected passed pawns supported by the king and bishop are too strong for him.

29 Kf2 Kg8 30 Ke3 Kf8 31 Kd4 Ke7 32 Kxd5 Ra8 33 Kc6 Rc8+ 34 Kb7 Rc5 35 Kb6 Rc3 36 Bc4 1-0

Black cannot stop the simple plan of a4-a5-a6-a7-a8Q and so resigns.

Conclusion

If Black does not play 3...Nd4!, I think White gets a very comfortable game. After taking on c6 to damage the black queenside, he can choose between targeting the weak pawns or going straight for the black king's throat, while Black's own counterplay is very slow. Against almost any set-up White can proceed with Bxc6, f2-f4, Nf3, d2-d3, 0-0 and Qe1-h4, when he has a ready-made attack and no weaknesses. The spoiler is 3...Na5!?, but then 4 Nf3 and d2-d4 gives White a promising Open Sicilian type position.

Chapter Seven

2...Nc6 3 Bb5 Nd4

The First Few Moves

Illustrative Games

Conclusion

The First Few Moves

1 e4 c5 2 Nc3 Nc6 3 Bb5 Nd4 (Diagram 1)

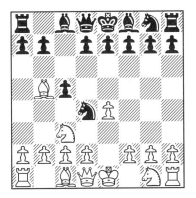

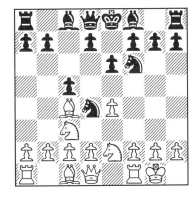

Diagram 1 (W)	**Diagram 2 (B)**
Black plays 3...Nd4	Position after 6 0-0

4 Bc4

NOTE: It may appear that Black has gained a tempo as the white bishop has spent two moves to reach c4. However, White can take advantage of the knight on d4 to speed his development.

4 Ba4 has also been played, notably by Armenian GMs Aronian and Petrosian, and may just transpose if Black responds with ...a7-a6 and ...b7-b5. All the same, I prefer bringing the bishop back to c4 so as to hit f7.

4...e6

The most logical move, blunting the bishop on c4. The main alternative, 4...g6 5 Nf3 Bg7 6 Nxd4! cxd4 7 Qf3!, is covered in Game 36.

5 Nge2

Slightly more accurate than 5 Nf3, which blocks the f-pawn and can also be pinned by the bishop on g4 in some lines.

5...Nf6

The other option is for the knight to go to e7 and then to c6. This set-up is examined in Games 34 and 35.

6 0-0 (Diagram 2) 6...a6

Instead:

a) 6...Nxe4?? fails due to 7 Nxe4 d5 8 Nxd4 cxd4 9 Bb5+ and White is a piece up.

b) 6...d5? is the obvious move, but it fails to a tactical trick: 7 exd5 exd5 8 Nxd5!, as seen in Game 33.

c) 6...b5!? is an old idea of Jonathan Rowson's, which was played against me by the super-GM Alexei Dreev at Gausdal 2007. I responded with the natural 7 Nxb5 Nxb5 8 Bxb5 Nxe4 9 d4, which has mostly been White's choice, but now I think 7 Nxd4! looks better. The game S.Movsesian-M.Krasenkow, Ostrava 2007, continued 7...bxc4 8 Nf3 d5 9 exd5 exd5 when, instead of 10 Re1+, the immediate 10 d4! should offer White a slight advantage.

7 d3 (Diagram 3)

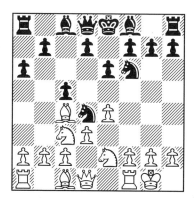

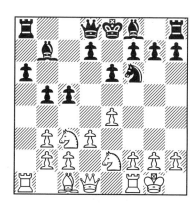

Diagram 3 (B)	**Diagram 4 (W)**
The 3 Bb5 main line	Position after 9...Bb7

7 a4 has also been played, but this allows 7...d5! as the temporary piece sacrifice no longer works: 8 exd5 exd5 9 Nxd5? Nxd5 10 Nxd4 cxd4 11 Qh5 and now 11...Be6 12 Re1 Nf4! since, in comparison with the 6...d5? line, there is no Bb5+ for White.

7...b5

This has developed into the main line of the 3 Bb5 variation. Note that 7...d5? fails again to 8 exd5 exd5 9 Nxd5! Nxd5 10 Nxd4 cxd4 11 Qh5. Here Spasov, a high-rated GM, tried 11...Ne7 (if 11...Be6 12 Re1 wins, as the c1-bishop prevents 12...Nf4), but lost quickly after 12 Qxf7+ Kd7 13 Re1 Kc6 14 Bg5! b5 15 Qf3+ 1-0 J.Radulski-V.Spasov, Bulgarian Championship 1994.

8 Bb3 Nxb3 9 axb3 Bb7 (Diagram 4)

I believe White has an advantage here. This position is the subject of the first game below.

Statistics

Bb5 is the best scoring line for White in the Grand Prix Attack. Even against the most critical reply, 3...Nd4, White achieves a healthy 56% with 413 wins and 302 losses from 1007 games in my database. In recent clashes between 2300+ players White has managed an even higher score with 61% from 235 games, winning 102 and losing just 52.

Illustrative Games

Game 32
□ **G.Jones** ■ **J.Sarkar**
Gibraltar 2007

1 e4 c5 2 Nc3 Nc6 3 Bb5 Nd4 4 Bc4 e6 5 Nge2 Nf6 6 0-0 a6 7 d3 b5 8 Bb3 Nxb3

8...Nc6!? is an interesting alternative. Black tries to prove that his knight is better than the bishop on b3. After 9 Bg5 Be7 10 f4 **(Diagram 5)** there is:

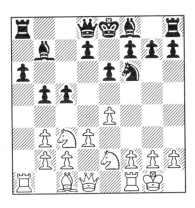

Diagram 5 (B)
The 8...Nc6!? variation

Diagram 6 (W)
White has three tries here

a) 10...c4 (or 10...b4 11 Na4) 11 dxc4 b4 12 Bxf6 Bxf6 13 Na4 and White is better; he might even consider 13 Nd5!?.

b) 10...Ng4 11 Bxe7 Qxe7 12 Qd2!? (12 Qe1 is the safer move) 12...c4 13 dxc4 bxc4 14 Ba4 (not 14 Bxc4? Qc5+) 14...Qc5+ 15 Kh1 Nf2+ 16 Rxf2 Qxf2 17 Bxc6 dxc6 18 Qd6 and White has very good compensation; e.g. 18...Qb6 19 Rd1 Ra7 20 Na4 Qa5 21 Qxc6+ Bd7 22 Qd6 Qc7 23 Qa3 now with a pawn for the exchange, while Black still cannot castle.

c) 10...h6 11 Bxf6 Bxf6 12 e5 Be7 13 a4 Rb8 (13...b4?! merely gifts White a nice outpost on c4 and drives his knight where it wants to go anyway) 14 axb5 axb5 15 Ne4 Bb7 16 c3 0-0 17 Kh1 d5 18 exd6 Bxd6 19 N2g3 Ne7 20 Qh5 Nd5 21 f5 (21 Bxd5! is slightly better for White) 21...Bxg3 22 fxe6!? Nf4 (22...c4! was preferable, when a complicated game ensues) 23 exf7+ Kh8 24 Qg4 c4?! (and here 24...Nxd3 2! Nxg3 c4 keeps the game alive) 25 Qxg3 Nh5 26 Qh3 cxb3 27 Qxh5 Qxd3 28 Nc5 Qc4? (Black had to try 28...Qd2, although 29 Qg4 should be winning; e.g. 29...Qxb? 30 Nxb7 Rxb7 31 Ra8!) 29 Rf6! 1-0 G.Jones-P.Wells, British League 2007. White threatens 30 Rxh6+, while if 29...Kh7 30 Qg6+ Kh8 31 Ne6 wins.

9 axb3 Bb7 (Diagram 6)

This is the critical line of the 3 Bb5 variation. Black has the two bishops, whilst White has the slightly easier development.

10 Bg5!?

I studied the position after Black's ninth move in depth and came to the conclusion that the text move, 10 Ng3 and 10 f4 are the most critical continuations. 10 Bg5!? had been played by Levon Aronian against Vallejo Pons in a rapid game (Monte Carlo 2006) and gave White a nice advantage (see below). Regarding the other two options:

a) 10 Ng3 supports f4-f5, but then 10...h5! is slightly annoying for White.

b) 10 f4 is probably more accurate; for example, if 10...d6 11 f5, or 10...Be7 11 Ng3!?, planning f4-f5, when 11...h5 can be answered by 12 e5!. Instead, 10...d5 11 e5 d4 12 exf6 dxc3 13 f5 Qxf6 14 fxe6 Qxe6 15 Nf4 Qd7 16 Re1+ Be7 17 Qe2 Kf8 18 bxc3 Re8 19 Qf2 was good for White in T.L.Petrosian-T.Kotanjian, Dubai 2007.

10...d6

10...h6!? 11 Bh4 g5! 12 Bg3 d6 is an interesting attempt at fighting back. For White 13 f3!? is probably best, intending to break in the centre with d3-d4 as Black has weakened himself on both flanks.

11 f4 Be7 12 f5

> **NOTE:** If the variation in the following note doesn't appeal to you, it's possible for White to play 12 Qe1 first (to cut out ...Nxe4 ideas) and then 13 f5, aiming for a position similar to the game.

12...e5

12...Nxe4!? was played in the aforementioned Aronian game, which continued 13 Bxe7 Nxc3 14 Bxd8 Nxd1 15 Bg5! Nxb2 16 Bc1 (trapping the knight) 16...Nxd3 17 cxd3 e5 and White had a slight advantage, as the knight is a bit better than the three pawns here, although Vallejo Pons made a draw.

13 Bxf6! Bxf6 (Diagram 7)

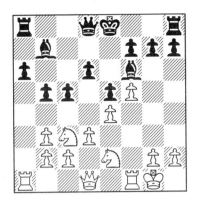

Diagram 7 (W)

The position favours the knights

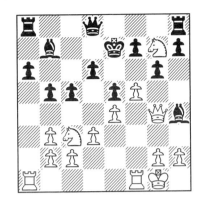

Diagram 8 (B)

White is clearly better

12...e5 gave away a nice outpost on d5 for a white knight, and if that is captured then the other knight will be able to go to e4. In this blocked position the knights are better than bishops.

14 Ng3 Bh4 15 Nh5 g6 16 Ng7+! Ke7

If 16...Kf8 17 fxg6! is very strong: Black cannot recapture the pawn due to 18 Ne6+ and so must take the knight, 17...Kxg7, but then 18 Rxf7+ picks up the b7-bishop and leaves Black's king stranded without any cover. 16...Kd7 17 fxg6 fxg6 18 Qg4+ Kc6 19 Rf7 is also very good for White.

17 Qf3?

This move throws away White's advantage. I should have played 17 Qg4! **(Diagram 8)**, as pointed out by IM Thomas Rendle after the game. Then 17...Bf6 (forced) 18 fxg6! hxg6 19 Qf3! Kf8 (Black cannot take the knight due to mate on f7) 20 Qxf6 Qxf6 21 Rxf6 Kxg7 22 Rxd6 (or first 22 Raf1) leaves White a pawn up in the ending.

17...Rg8 18 f6+

I could have tried 18 Nd5+!? Bxd5 19 exd5, hoping for 19...Rxg7? 20 f6+ Bxf6 21 Qxf6+ Kf8 22 Rxa6!!, exploiting the undefended position of the black queen. But after 19...Kd7! there is nothing better than 20 Ne6 fxe6 21 dxe6+ Kc7 22 f6 Bxf6! 23 Qxf6 Qxf6 24 Rxf6 Rge8 when Black is fine.

18...Kf8 19 Nd5 Bxd5 20 exd5 Bxf6 21 Ne6+ fxe6 22 Qxf6+ Qxf6 23 Rxf6+ Ke7 24 Rxe6+ Kd7 (Diagram 9)

We've reached an equal ending which should obviously end as a draw, but I was annoyed at throwing away the advantage and decided to carry on playing, trying to show that a6 is a weakness. This endgame really goes beyond the scope of this book, but I'll give a few notes anyway.

25 Rf6 Ke7 26 Raf1 Rgf8 27 Rxf8 Rxf8 28 Ra1!

Forcing Black's rook to go passive.

28...Ra8 29 Kf2 a5 30 Ke3 h5 31 g3 b4

It might have been better to leave the pawn on b5, so that ...a5-a4 could be played at some point to try and swap the pawns that way.

32 h3 Kd7 33 Ke4 Ke7

I can't make any more improvements to my position, so I change my attack from the weak a5-pawn to the d6-pawn.

34 c3 Rb8 35 Rxa5 bxc3 36 bxc3 Rxb3 37 Ra7+ Kf6 38 Rd7!

Forcing the black rook to remain passive.

38...Rb6 39 h4 Ra6 (Diagram 10)

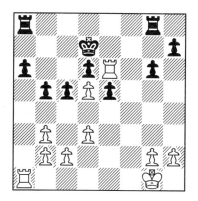

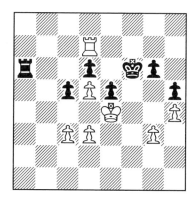

Diagram 9 (W)	Diagram 10 (W)
An equal ending	Only White can win

With slightly safer pawns and more active pieces, White is the only one who can win this position. Black should be able to hold the draw, but it still requires accurate defence.

40 Kf3 Rb6 41 c4 Ra6 42 g4 hxg4+ 43 Kxg4 Rb6 44 Kf3 Ra6 45 Ke3 Rb6 46 Kd2 e4?!

Black gets bored of being passive. Perhaps he saw some ghosts where my king came to a5 to dislodge the rook from its defence of d6, but after the correct 46...Rb2+! 47 Kc3 Rb6 48 Kc2 Ra6 49 Kb3 Kf5! 50 Rf7+ Kg4 51 Rf6 Kh5 White can't make any progress.

47 dxe4 Ke5 48 Rg7

Attacking the g-pawn in order to create a passed pawn.

48...Kd4 49 Rxg6 Rb2+ 50 Ke1! (Diagram 11)

Diagram 11 (B)

The decisive moment

Diagram 12 (B)

White is winning

If 50 Kc1 Re2 51 h5 Rxe4 52 Rxd6 Rh4 53 h6 Kxc4 draws, while 50 Kd1 Kxc4 51 Rxd6 Kd3 is even dangerous, as Black now has a passed pawn of his own and mating threats.

50...Kxe4?

The losing move. 50...Kxc4 51 Rxd6 Kd3 was still correct, and if 52 Re6 c4 53 d6 c3 54 d7 Ke3! 55 d8Q Rb1+ 56 Qd1 c2! forces 57 Rd6 Rxd1+ 58 Rxd1 cxd1Q+ 59 Kxd1 Kxe4 and draws.

51 Rxd6 Kd4 52 Re6 Rb7

Now if 52...Kxc4 53 d6 does win; e.g. 53...Rb7 54 Re7 Rb8 55 d7 Rd8 56 h5 Kd5 57 h6 Kd6 58 Rg7 Kc7 59 h7 Rh8 60 Rg8 etc.

53 d6 Rd7 54 h5 Kxc4 55 h6 Rh7

Or 55...Kd5 56 Re2! and the d-pawn is invulnerable due to Rd2+.

56 Re2! (Diagram 12)

Reorganizing so I can play Rd2 and d6-d7, while if 56...Kd5 57 d7! wins at once.

56...Rxh6 57 d7 Rh8 58 Re8 Rh1+ 59 Kf2 Rh2+ 60 Kg3 Rd2 61 d8Q Rxd8 62 Rxd8

White's king is easily near enough to stop the pawn.

62...Kb3 63 Kf2 c4 64 Ke2 Kc2 65 Rc8 c3 66 Rc7 Kb2 67 Kd3 1-0

Game 33
☐ **G.Jones** ■ **F.Nijboer**
Groningen 2004

I played this game in a strong grandmaster tournament and had had a rotten start with 0/5. I'd also had a bad night's sleep and in fact only woke up when the arbiter phoned my room to enquire why I wasn't at the board! I stumbled downstairs feeling awful, and around forty minutes behind on the clock, so I decided to play something I knew well...

1 e4 c5 2 Nc3 Nc6 3 Bb5 Nd4 4 Bc4 e6 5 Nge2 Nf6 6 0-0 d5?

The natural move for Black, but it falls for a nice trick.

7 exd5 exd5 8 Nxd5!! (Diagram 13)

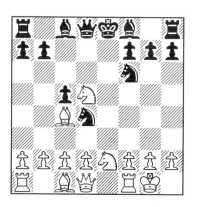

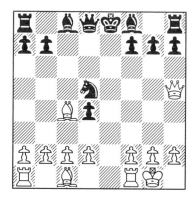

Diagram 13 (B)

A nice trick

Diagram 14 (B)

The knight is pinned to f7

8...Nxd5

As Black can't keep the extra piece in any case he has also tried 8...Nf3+, hoping to destroy White's pawn structure and weaken his king. But after 9 Kh1! (9 gxf3 Nxd5 isn't as clear) 9...Nxd5 10 Nc3!! (hitting the d5-knight and threatening to take on f3 with the queen) 10...Nxc3?! (if 10...Nd4 11 Bxd5 and White is simply a pawn up) 11 Qxf3 (threatening mate on f7, so Black cannot defend his knight) 11...Qe7 12 dxc3, White keeps his kingside pawn structure intact, wins back the piece, and will be a pawn up with the initiative. Actually he is pretty much winning here.

9 Nxd4 cxd4 10 Qh5! (Diagram 14)

The point. The black knight cannot move without allowing White to take on f7.

10...Be7

Nothing else is really much better:

a) 10...Be6 11 Re1 and the pins on the e-file and h5-a8 diagonal ensure that White will regain the piece on either e6 or d5; for example, 11...Be7 12 Rxe6, 11...Nc7 12 Bxe6, or 11...g6 12 Qe5 Rg8 13 Bxd5.

b) 10...g5 11 Re1+ Be7 12 d3 with a winning attack. Black's position has too many holes.

c) 10...Ne7 11 Qxf7+ Kd7 12 Re1 and White has a huge attack and two pawns for the piece. Indeed, *Fritz* gives White a clear advantage here. A sample line might run 12...Kc6 13 a4 a6 14 b4 Kb6 15 a5+ Ka7 16 b5 axb5 17 Bxb5 Kb8 18 a6 bxa6 19 Ba3 axb5 20 Qf4+ Kb7 21 Bxe7 Bxe7 22 Qe4+ Kc7 23 Rxa8 when White levels the point count while retaining the attack.

11 Qxd5 0-0 12 Qxd8 Rxd8 13 Re1 (Diagram 15)

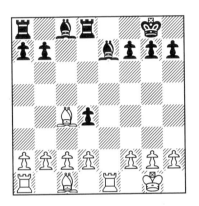

Diagram 15 (B)

Black is a pawn down

Diagram 16 (B)

White has consolidated

Black is a pawn down in a queenless middlegame position and is objectively lost. He now tries sacrificing another pawn in order to get some counterplay, but it is never enough.

13...Be6!? 14 Bxe6 fxe6 15 Rxe6 Kf7 16 Re2 d3 17 cxd3 Rac8

Here I decided to return two of my extra three pawns so that I could complete my development.

18 d4! Rxd4 19 d3! Rxd3 20 Be3 a5 21 Kf1 Rc6 22 Ree1 Bf6 23 Rad1 Rxd1 24 Rxd1 Ke6

If 24...Bxb2 25 Rd7+ Ke6 26 Rxb7 Rc2 27 Ra7 Bc3 28 Rc7 leaves White a pawn up again with a clear advantage.

25 b3 Rc2 26 Rd2 Rc1+ 27 Ke2 Rg1 28 Kf3 (Diagram 16)

Having finally consolidated my extra pawn I now went on to win.

28...b5 29 Re2 Kf5 30 Bd2 g5 31 h3 h5 32 Re4 Ra1 33 g4+ hxg4+ 34 hxg4+ Kg6 35 Re6 b4 36 Be3 Rd1 37 Ra6 Rd5 38 Ke4 Re5+ 39 Kd3 1-0

Game 34
☐ G.Jones ■ M.Devereaux
British Championship, Swansea 2006

1 e4 c5 2 Nc3 Nc6 3 Bb5 Nd4 4 Bc4 e6 5 Nge2 a6 6 d3

6 Nxd4 is possible straight away, but I prefer waiting with 6 d3.

6...Ne7 7 0-0 (Diagram 17)

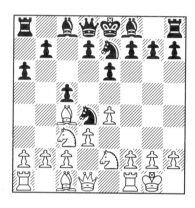
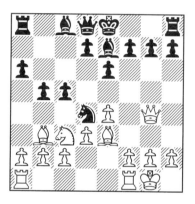

Diagram 17 (B)

Position after 7 0-0

Diagram 18 (B)

Black lags in development

7...b5

Instead:

a) 7...Nec6 8 Nxd4 Nxd4 will probably transpose to the game; e.g. after 9 Be3 b5 10 Bb3.

b) 7...d5? falls for the now familiar trick: 8 exd5 exd5 9 Nxd5!! Nxd5 10 Nxd4 cxd4 11 Qh5 etc.

c) 7...g6 8 Bg5 Bg7 9 Nxd4 cxd4 10 Ne2 0-0 11 Qd2 b5 12 Bb3 Bb7 13 a4 f6 14 Bf4 f5 15 Bd6 was good for White in G.Jones-I.Snape, British League 2006.

8 Bb3 Nec6

8...Nxb3 9 axb3 is similar to Game 32, but with his knight on e7 (rather than f6) it's harder for Black to develop, so White has at least a slight edge.

9 Nxd4 Nxd4

After 9...cxd4 10 Ne2 White has nice attacking chances with f2-f4-f5 coming swiftly.

10 Be3

This time I decided to develop my pieces before committing to f2-f4.

10...Be7 11 Qg4! (Diagram 18) 11...h5?!

Afraid of the attack Black decides to jettison his g7-pawn to try to get some counterplay, but White just emerges a pawn up, while Black now has no safe square for his king.

Instead, the solid 11...0-0 looks best, but after 12 Bxd4! (not 12 Bh6 Bf6 13 f4 Kh8 and White cannot break through) 12...cxd4 13 Ne2 Qb6 14 f4! White again has a swift attack, while Black is yet to complete his development.

12 Qxg7 Bf6 13 Qg3 d6

13...b4 is answered by 14 Bxd4 (14 Na4?? drops the queen to 14...Ne2+) 14...Bxd4 15 Nd1 with a clear advantage.

14 Bxd4

Getting rid of Black's strong knight and thereby ruling out any ...Ne2+ tricks.

14...cxd4

14...Bxd4 is probably slightly better, but White still has a clear edge after 15 Nd1! followed by c2-c3, Ne3 and perhaps eventually d3-d4.

15 Ne2 h4 16 Qf3

Threatening 17 e5 winning a piece.

16...Bb7 17 c3 dxc3 18 bxc3 Rc8

If 18...h3 then simply 19 g3 and White's king is perfectly safe.

19 d4 (Diagram 19)

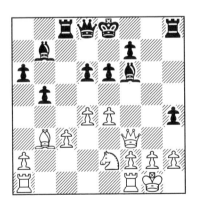

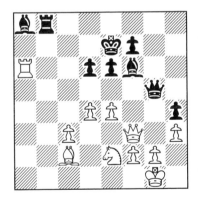

Diagram 19 (B)	Diagram 20 (B)
Black is virtually lost	The result is not in doubt

Here White is basically winning. He has more space, a strong centre, a safer king, and is a pawn up!

19...Ke7 20 a4!

Targeting Black's queenside pawns.

20...bxa4 21 Rxa4 Qg8 22 Rb4 Ba8 23 Ra1 Qg6 24 Bc2 Qg5 25 h3 Rb8 26 Rxb8 Rxb8 27 Rxa6 (Diagram 20)

White wins a second pawn and still has all his positional trumps.

27...Qd2 28 Ra7+ Rb7 29 Rxa8 Qxc2 30 e5 Qb1+ 31 Kh2 dxe5 32 Qc6 Bg7 33 Rg8 Kf6 34 Qf3+ Qf5 35 Qxb7 e4 36 Qc7 1-0

Game 35
□ **B.Spassky** ■ **G.Kasparov**
Reykjavik World Cup 1988

In this game between two former World Champions (Kasparov had won the championship a couple of years earlier), White achieves a good position out of the opening, but accepts a draw from his high-rated opponent.

1 e4 c5 2 Nc3 Nc6 3 Bb5 Nd4 4 Bc4 e6 5 Nf3

Personally I prefer 5 Nge2, since if Black plays in the same fashion as Game 32 then White's knight is better placed on e2, from where it can jump to g3 and does not block the f-pawn.

5...Ne7 6 0-0

6 Nxd4 cxd4 7 Ne2 immediately might be more accurate, cutting out Black's option of recapturing with the knight, but the lines will often transpose; for instance, 7...Nc6 8 d3 g6 9 0-0 joins the game at move nine.

6...Nec6 (Diagram 21)

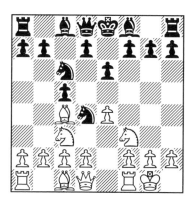
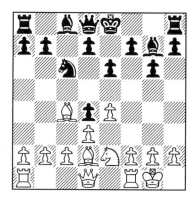

Diagram 21 (W)
Black strongpoints d4

Diagram 22 (B)
An interesting idea

7 d3

The position is similar to the previous game, and if Black now played 7...a6 it would probably transpose; i.e. after 8 Nxd4 Nxd4 9 Be3 b5 10 Bb3.

7...g6

7...Nxf3 8 Qxf3 Nd4 9 Qd1 comes to the same thing as recapturing on d4 with the knight, as in the next note.

8 Nxd4 cxd4

After 8...Nxd4 White can exchange the other pair of knights as well: 9 Ne2 Nxe2+ 10 Qxe2 Bg7 11 c3 (11 Bf4!? also comes into consideration) 11...0-0 12 e5 with the advantage.

9 Ne2 Bg7 10 Bd2!? (Diagram 22)

An interesting idea by the tenth World Champion. 10 f4 would be the normal plan, but then Black has the reply 10...d5! 11 Bb3 (11 exd5 exd5 sees Black doing well, as his doubled pawns control many important squares, whereas White's f2-f4 now gets in the way and has left weaknesses behind, such as on e3) 11...0-0 12 Ng3, although White can perhaps claim a small edge.

10...0-0

Now if 10...d5?! 11 exd5 exd5 12 Bb3 0-0 13 Nf4 targets the d5-pawn immediately.

11 b4!?

We see the point of 10 Bd2. Recapturing on d4 with the c-pawn has meant that Black has weakened his queenside control, so Spassky grabs space there.

11...b6 12 b5 Ne7 13 Bb4 d6 14 a4 a5

Otherwise White plays a4-a5 himself and gets a lot of pressure down the a-file.

15 Ba3 Bb7 16 Bb3

A familiar prophylactic retreat. White doesn't want to be bothered with ...d6-d5 some time in the future, or even immediately.

16...d5 17 f3!? (Diagram 23)

17 exd5 Nxd5! would be in Kasparov's style, sacrificing the exchange for the initiative when his two bishops would dominate the board and White's pieces are slightly passive. Understandably Spassky prefers to maintain the pressure.

17...Qc7 18 Qe1!

Bringing the queen to her usual active post on h4.

18...Rad8 19 Qh4 (Diagram 24) ½-½

A rather disappointing end to the game. White has achieved a slight, but enduring advantage out of the opening with more space and better placed pieces, in particular the bishop on a3. I'm sure that if Spassky had been playing someone weaker than himself he might well have continued here, but a draw with Kasparov is a good result!

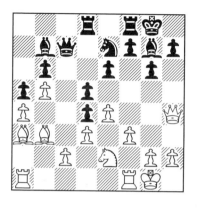

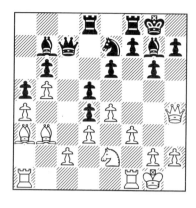

Diagram 23 (B)
Maintaining the centre

Diagram 24 (B)
White is slightly better

Game 36
□ **P.Svidler** ■ **P.Leko**
Dortmund 2004

1 e4 c5 2 Nc3 Nc6 3 Bb5 Nd4 4 Bc4 g6

> **NOTE: This line used to be very topical and featured in several clashes between the World's top grandmasters. Nowadays Black has more or less abandoned 4...g6 at the highest level, because of games such as this one, and switched to the lines we've examined earlier in the chapter.**

5 Nf3

Against 4...g6 it doesn't really make any difference whether you play 5 Nge2 or 5 Nf3 as you are going to capture on d4 next move.

5...Bg7 6 Nxd4! cxd4 7 Qf3! (Diagram 25)

This makes it awkward for Black to complete his development and, while looking crude, offers White a nice game.

7...Nh6

An almost forced move, but very difficult to play if Black does not know the theory. Instead:

a) 7...Nf6 8 Nb5 0-0 9 Nxd4 and although Black has some activity, White has an extra pawn and should be able to consolidate with due care and attention; for example, 9...d5 10 exd5 e5 11 Ne2 Bg4 12 Qg3 Rc8 13 d3 b5 14 Bb3 Bxe2 15 Kxe2

Nxd5 16 Re1 Nb6 17 Bd2 e4 18 dxe4 Bxb2 19 Rad1 Qe7 20 Kf1 and White went on to win in I.Ibragimov-E.Real de Azua, Buenos Aires 2005.

b) 7...e6? 8 Nb5 d6 (8...d5 might be the best try here; after 9 exd5 a6 10 dxe6 fxe6 11 Na3 Nf6 White is a pawn up and e6 is weak, but the knight is misplaced on a3 so Black has some slim practical chances) 9 Qa3! **(Diagram 26)** and Black encounters severe problems in keeping his d-pawns:

Diagram 25 (B)

White attacks f7

Diagram 26 (B)

Now d6 is the target

b1) 9...Bf8 10 Nxd4 just drops a pawn.

b2) 9...Be5 10 0-0 and Black is in a lot of trouble with f2-f4 threatened; e.g. 10...g5 (or 10...Qh4 11 f4 Bxf4 12 g3) 11 d3 a6 12 Bxg5! Qxg5 13 Nc7+ and 14 Nxa8 wins.

b3) 9...Ke7 10 c3 dxc3, when White can either recapture on c3 or just castle. I have had this position twice and won quickly on both occasions. Black's king is stuck in the middle and he has huge problems developing his pieces as ...Nf6 is met by e4-e5. For example, 11 0-0!? (11 dxc3 also gives White a huge advantage) 11...a6 12 Nxc3 Qc7 13 d3 Bd7 14 Bf4 Qc5 15 b4 Qh5 16 d4 Rc8 17 Be2 Rxc3 18 Qb2 Qh4 19 g3 Qf6 20 e5 1-0 G.Jones-L.Camerini, Montecatini Terme 2003.

8 Ne2

I prefer this move order to the immediate 8 d3, as apart from 8...0-0 (not 8...dxc3? 9 Bxh6 Bxh6? 10 Qxf7 mate) 9 Ne2 transposing to the game, Black can also play 8...Qa5!? with the following forced variation: 9 Bxh6 Bxh6 10 Qxf7+ Kd8 11 Qd5 Qxd5 12 Nxd5 e6 13 Nf6 (not 13 Nb4? a5 trapping the knight) 13...Bg7 14 e5 (and not 14 Ng4? h5 – a nice reflection!) when 14...Bxf6 15 exf6 Rf8 regains the pawn, M.Zufic-V.Malakhov, Bled 2001.

8...0-0 9 d3

9 Bb3!? is also interesting and was the move I played last time I reached this posi-

tion. That game continued 9...e6 (9...d6 10 d3 Ng4 returns to the main line) 10 d3 f5 11 Bxh6?! (11 Qg3 was correct, with a slight advantage) 11...Bxh6 12 Nxd4 fxe4 13 Qxe4 Qf6?! (13...Rf4! would have been a little unpleasant) 14 Nf3 Qxb2 15 0-0 a5 16 a4 Bg7 17 d4 Qc3 18 d5 Ra6 19 Rad1 and White was now clearly better in G.Jones-E.Wiersma, European Club Cup, Fuegen 2006.

9...Ng4!

Black's trump move, otherwise he would be a lot worse.

10 Bb3!

10 Qxg4?! d5! and 11...dxc4 gives Black good compensation, with the two bishops, better pawn structure and more active pieces.

10...d6 11 Qg3 (Diagram 27)

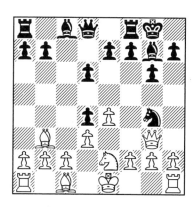

Diagram 27 (B)

Getting ready to attack

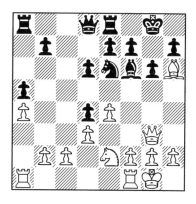

Diagram 28 (B)

Black needs quick counterplay

Manoeuvring the queen to her usual position on h4 and giving White the option of a quick attack in the true Grand Prix style with f4-f5, especially if Black plays ...Ne5.

11...a5 12 a4 Nf6 13 0-0

13 Nxd4 is also possible. After 13...Nxe4 14 dxe4 Bxd4 15 0-0 White has a slight advantage with a lead in development and more active pieces. Instead, Svidler prefers to keep the position more closed for the moment and leaves the d4-pawn as a possible weakness for later in the game

13...Nd7 14 Bg5

Developing the bishop and targeting the weak e7-square.

14...Nc5 15 Qh4 Re8

Black doesn't have time to take on b3: if 15...Nxb3? 16 Bxe7 Qb6 17 cxb3 Re8 18 Bf6 and White is clearly better.

16 Bd5 Be6

With the more passive position Black swaps off pieces to ease his defence.

17 Bxe6 Nxe6 18 Bh6 Bf6

Black cannot, however, allow these bishops to be swapped off as it would weaken his kingside too much: 18...Bxh6 19 Qxh6 Qb6 20 f4!? (20 Rab1 is also possible, simply keeping the queenside under control) 20...Qxb2 21 f5 Nc5? 22 Nf4 gives White a winning attack; e.g. 22...Qxc2 23 Rf3 (threatening 24 Rh3) 23...Nd7 24 Nh5! and mates.

19 Qg3 (Diagram 28)

We've reached an interesting position. White has his pieces ready to start a quick kingside assault, so Black needs to find counterplay by quickly targeting the white queenside, in particular the vulnerable c2-pawn, which is held backward on the half-open c-file by the black pawn on d4.

 WARNING: 19 Qg4! is probably more accurate here, as after 19 Qg3 Black has 19...Qb6! 20 b3 Qc5!, threatening both 21...Qxc2 and the sneaky 21...Qh5 forking the bishop and knight – as occurred after 21 Ra2? Qh5 in O.Sabirova-V.Cmilyte, Turin Olympiad 2006.

With the white queen on g4 Black does not have this trick, while 19...Rc8 20 Rac1 Qb6 21 b3 Rc5 22 f4 Rh5 23 f5 Rh4 24 Qg3 Rxh6 transposes to the game.

19...Rc8 20 Rac1 Qb6 21 b3 Rc5!

Threatening to double on the c-file, with the added idea of swinging the rook across to h5 to defend the kingside.

22 f4

Svidler keeps on with his attack. Now if 22...Rec8 23 f5 Ng7 24 Nf4 Rxc2 25 Rxc2 Rxc2 26 Nd5 gives White huge compensation for the pawn with his great knight on d5 controlling the board, so Leko switches over to defence.

22...Rh5 23 f5

Forced, since the bishop on h6 is trapped.

23...Rxh6

23...Nc5?! 24 Bd2 would leave the rook looking rather offside on h5 and short of squares.

24 fxe6 fxe6 25 Nf4 (Diagram 29)

For the sacrificed pawn White has good play on the light squares, while Black's forces are all rather disconnected – the h6-rook in particular is hardly contributing much, being stupidly placed on the edge of the board.

25 Nf4 Qc5

Black elects not to defend his extra pawn anyway, as he decides White's initiative would be too great. For example, after 25...e5 26 Nd5 Qd8 27 Qg4 Bg7 28 Qe6+ Kh8 29 Rf7 White has easily enough compensation for the sacrificed pawn.

26 Nxe6 Qe5 27 Qxe5 Bxe5 28 g3 (Diagram 30)

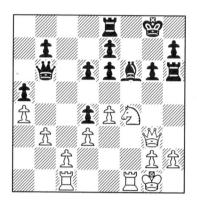
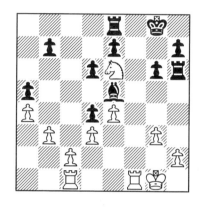

Diagram 29 (B)

Play on the light squares

Diagram 30 (B)

White is clearly better

The trade of queens has stopped White's attack, but he still has a clear advantage thanks to his great knight outpost on e6, the open f-file and the extremely passive nature of the black rooks. He also has the superior structure, with just the c2-pawn as a possible weakness, whereas Black's three pawn islands are potentially far more vulnerable.

28...Rh5

Trying to activate that sorry-looking rook, but perhaps he should have preferred 28...Rc8 to prevent White's next move.

29 c3! dxc3 30 d4 Bf6 31 Rxc3

White has eliminated his only pawn weakness and taken over the c-file. Now all White's pieces are active and he has a decisive advantage.

Kf7 32 Nc7

32 d5!?, maintaining the knight on e6, also required consideration, but Svidler decides he doesn't want Black's bishop on f6 to become active.

32...Rc8 33 Kg2

Here 33 Rc4 might be more accurate, not allowing Black's defensive try. Then if 33...Kg8 34 Ne6! defends the d-pawn.

33...Kg8

Unpinning the bishop and hitting d4.

34 Rd1 Rc5!

A neat trick, by which Black swaps off a pair of rooks and activates his bishop.

35 dxc5 Bxc3 36 cxd6 exd6 37 Nb5 Be5 (Diagram 31)

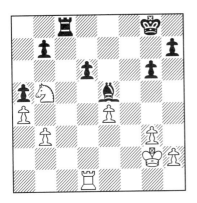 

Diagram 31 (W)
The knight is still strong

Diagram 32 (B)
White's pawns are faster

White's advantage has decreased somewhat, but he still has a strong knight with outposts at b5 and c4, while Black's queenside pawns are all weak.

38 Rd5

Not 38 Nxd6?? Rd8 winning a piece.

38...Rc6?!

Black's best chance was to go for active counterplay at once with 38...Rc2+ and 39...Rb2, but quite likely Leko was short of time at this point.

39 Na3!

Relocating the knight to c4 where it can hit a5, d6 and e5.

39...Rc3 40 Rb5!

Defending b3 and attacking b7.

40...Re3 41 Nc4 Rxe4 42 Nxa5 Re2+ 43 Kf3 Rxh2 44 Nc4 Bd4 45 Rxb7 (Diagram 32)

Material might be equal, but White now has a winning advantage with two connected passed pawns and the more active king.

45...d5 46 Ne3 h5 47 Nxd5 g5 48 a5 Ra2 49 b4 h4 50 gxh4?!

It is hard to be accurate at the end of a game. Here 50 Kg4! was correct, and if 50...Rg2 51 Kh5 Rxg3 52 Kg6 mates, or 50...hxg3 51 Kxg3 and the remaining black pawn won't last long on g5.

50...gxh4 51 Kg4 Bf2 52 Kg5!?

After the logical 52 Ne7+ Kf8 53 Nc6 Be1! it is not so easy for White to advance his pawns further, while Black might play ...Ra3 and ...h4-h3. So instead Svidler tries for a mating net.

52...Kf8 53 Nf6 Ra3?

The losing move. Not 53...h3? 54 Kg6 and there's no defence to Rf7 mate, but 53...Bd4 might still have held on; e.g. 54 Nd7+ Ke8 55 Kxh4 Bc3! (intending 56...Bxb4 57 Rxb4 Rxa5) 56 Nb8 Bxb4 57 a6 Bd6 58 a7 Bc5! with a draw.

54 Ng4 Be1 55 Kf6 Bc3+ 56 Ne5 Kg8 57 Rg7+ Kh8 58 Rg4 h3 59 Kf7!

Closing the trap.

59...Be1 60 Rg7 1-0

There is no good defence to 61 Ng6 mate.

Conclusion

2 Nc3 Nc6 3 Bb5 is an interesting line which is becoming more and more popular. After 3...Nd4 4 Bc4 the main line used to be 4...g6, but around 2003/04 White began scoring very heavily and since then its popularity has inevitably suffered. Nowadays 4...e6 is Black's favoured response, when I think 5 Nge2 Nf6 6 0-0 a6 7 d3 b5 8 Bb3 Nxb3 9 axb3 Bb7 is critical, as in the game Jones-Sarkar (Game 32). Here White has a choice between 10 Bg5, 10 f4 and 10 Ng3, all of which lead to interesting play.

Index of Variations

Chapter One

1 e4 c5 2 Nc3 Nc6 3 f4 g6
    3...e6 – *see Chapter Four*
4 Nf3 Bg7 5 Bc4

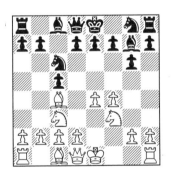

5...e6
    5...d6 – *see Chapter Three*
6 f5
    6 0-0 – *25*
6...Nge7
    6...gxf5 – *16*
7 fxe6 dxe6 – *18*
    7...fxe6 – *21*

Chapter Two

1 e4 c5 2 Nc3 Nc6 3 f4 g6 4 Nf3 Bg7 5 Bb5

5...Nd4 6 0-0

   6 Bd3 – *60*

6...Nxb5

   6...e6 – *48*

   6...a6 7 Bd3

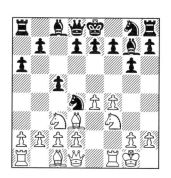

   7...d6 – *52*

   7...b5 – *57*

7 Nxb5 d5

   7...d6

      8 d4 – *40*

      8 d3 – *43*

8 exd5 – *32*

   8 e5 – *36*

Chapter Three

1 e4 c5 2 Nc3 d6 3 f4 g6 4 Nf3 Bg7 5 Bc4 Nc6 6 0-0

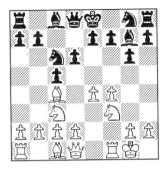

6...e6

    6...Nf6 – *83*

7 d3 Nge7 8 Qe1 0-0

    8...h6 – *77*

9 f5 – *70*

    9 a3 – *75*

Chapter Four

1 e4 c5 2 Nc3 e6 3 f4

3...Nc6

    3...d5 4 Nf3 dxe4 5 Nxe4

        5...Nd7 – *104*

        5...Nc6 – *109*

4 Nf3

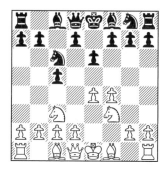

4...a6
> 4...d5 – *90*
> 4...d6 – *101*

5 g3 – *95*
> 5 Be2 – *99*

Chapter Five

1 e4 c5 2 Nc3 a6

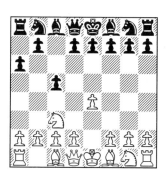

> 2...g6 – *122*
> 2...b6 – *124*

3 f4 b5 – *116*
> 3...d6 – *119*

Chapter Six

1 e4 c5 2 Nc3 Nc6 3 Bb5

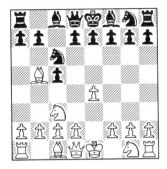

3...g6
    3...d6 – *131*
    3...Na5 – *142*
4 Bxc6 bxc6
    4...dxc6

    5 f4 – *138*
    5 d3 – *140*
5 f4 Bg7 6 Nf3 d6 – *131*
    6...Nh6 – *133*

Chapter Seven

1 e4 c5 2 Nc3 Nc6 3 Bb5 Nd4 4 Bc4

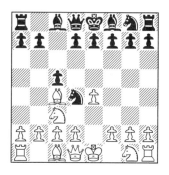

4...e6

    4...g6 – *160*

5 Nge2

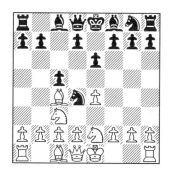

5...Nf6

    5...a6 – *156*

    5...Ne7 – *158*

6 0-0 a6 – *149*

    6...d5 – *153*

Index of Complete Games

Adams.M-Anand.V, *FIDE World Championship, Groningen 1997* 52

Anand.V-Gelfand.B, *Wijk aan Zee 1996* 77

Benjamin.J-Smith.B, *Philadelphia World Open 2006* 32

Chandler.M-Schenk.A, *British League 2006* 75

Ekebjaerg.O-Lundholm.S, *Correspondence 1989* 95

Giorgadze.G-Corral Blanco.J, *Spanish Team Championship 2003* 25

Giorgadze.G-Kouatly.B, *Manila Olympiad 1992* 109

Harikrishna.P-Bu Xiangzhi, *Tiayuan 2005* 116

Hernandez.Gil-Minzer.C, *Mislata 2000* 131

Iuldachev.S-El Arousy.A, *Abu Dhabi 2003* 90

Ivanov.Alexa-Abeln.M, *Dutch Open Championship 1992* 18

Jones.G-Agopov.M, *European Team Championship, Crete 2007* 43

Jones.G-Arakhamia.K, *British League 2006* 101

Jones.G-Devereaux.M, *British Championship, Swansea 2006* 156

Jones.G-Eppinger.G, *Calvia 2006* 138

Jones.G-Gelashvili.T, *European Team Championship, Crete 2007* 48

Jones.G-Horvath.Ad, *European Club Cup, Fuegen 2006* 142

Jones.G-Nijboer.F, *Groningen 2004* 153

Jones.G-Sarkar.J, *Gibraltar 2007* 149

Jones.G-Stojanovski.D, *Pula 2007* 133

Jones.G-Van Wely.L, *Staunton Memorial, London 2007* 57

Kosten.A-Arakhamia.K, *Aosta 1990* 124

Lobron.E-Andruet.G, *Marseilles 1989* 119

Lutton.J.E-Dougherty.M, *Isle of Man 2002* 99

Macieja.B-Haznedaroglu.K, *European Championship, Antalya 2004* 140

Macieja.B-Wells.P, *European Championship, Warsaw 2005* 39

Meister.Y-Manik.M, *Pardubice 1995* 16

Minasian.Art-Petrosian.T.A, *Yerevan 2004* 36

Mitkov.N-Alvarez.Joh, *Istanbul Olympiad 2000* 83

Najer.E-Kron.V, *Moscow 1998* 122

Paschall.W-Bakre.T, *Budapest 2001* 21

Polgar.J-Topalov.V, *Dortmund 1996* 60

Short.N-Oll.L, *Tallinn 1998* 70

Spassky.B-Kasparov.G, *Reykjavik World Cup 1988* 158

Svidler.P-Leko.P, *Dortmund 2004* 160

Tiviakov.S-Kurnosov.I, *European Championship, Istanbul 2003* 104